The Mirror Of Existence

Also by Christine Page

Frontiers of Health

The Mirror Of Existence

STEPPING INTO WHOLENESS

DR CHRISTINE R. PAGE

MBBS, MRCGP, DCH, DRCOG, MFHom

Index compiled by
Lyn Greenwood

SAFFRON WALDEN
THE C.W. DANIEL COMPANY LIMITED

First published in Great Britain in 1995
by The C.W. Daniel Company Limited
1 Church Path, Saffron Walden
Essex, CB10 1JP, England

© Christine R. Page 1995
illustrations © Sonia Fynn 1995

ISBN 0 85207 294 5

This book has been printed on environmentally friendly paper

Reprinted 1997

Designed and produced in
association with Book Production Consultants plc,
Typeset by Cambridge Photosetting Services
Printed and Bound by WSOY, Finland

DEDICATION

To those who live and walk in the Light

Contents

ACKNOWLEDGEMENTS

Illustrations by Sonia Fynn.
Proof reading by Pat Jarvis.
Grateful thanks to both.

Chapter 1

Stepping Into Life

A friend of mine agreed to look after his three-year old nephew for the afternoon whilst the child's parents were away. In preparation, he gathered together an assortment of his own old toys which he thought the boy would like to play with during his stay.

As is the way with children, the nephew completely ignored his Uncle's memorabilia and spent most of his time fascinated by a large standing mirror in the bedroom.

He stood in front of it, to the side of it, with his back to it and even behind it.

Finally, just before tea, he ran to his Uncle with a look of great pleasure and excitement.

"Unc" he said, with child-like familiarity, "Unc, do you know that wherever I stand around the mirror I can only see part of me?"

And then with an enormous sigh of satisfaction he concluded: "It is only when I step into the mirror can I see all of me!

Out of the mouth of babes the truth is told.

All life is a mirror reflecting our inner thoughts and inspirations. However, this mirror is unique for it has magical properties which allow us to step inside and become active participants in our own creative process.

In order to do this, we have to be willing to let go of some of our individuality so that we may interact freely with situations and people that we may meet along the way.

For some individuals, such loss of identity threatens their security and they choose to stand on the outside, projecting relatively limited thoughts into the mirror and receiving predictable reflections. They hold onto dogmatic beliefs which structure their identity, fearful of losing themselves within a crowd.

Diagram 1

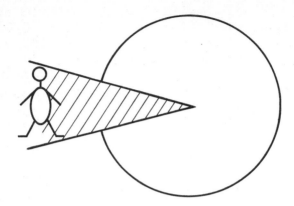

Unfortunately such security is gained at the expense of connection, both with themselves and with others, leading to feelings of isolation and rejection. Eventually they come to realise that true security is not gained by remaining separate but by the ability to integrate fully with the world whilst maintaining their own integrity.

Then there are those who willingly step inside the mirror recognising that only by accepting the need to change will they grow. They happily release their need to be separate and engage in the situations which come towards them.

However, once inside it is easy to lose all sense of boundaries and these individuals then become immersed within the drama of life forgetting their spiritual origins and reacting purely to feelings rather than to their higher wisdom. Now the emotions have become the driving force which formulates the next action. Emotions attracting emotions. Fear attracting fear.

Diagram 2

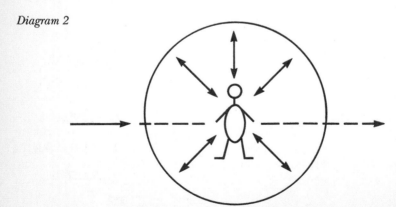

Their salvation is to have the courage to step out of the mirror, often against the tide of general opinion, guided only by a distant memory of their own inner truth. With this step tremendous transformation takes place creating a wonderful sense of inner peace and security.

Finally, there are those who unconsciously step inside the mirror, interact with situations they meet and step out again without ever acknowledging that they are the creators of their own reality.

Diagram 3

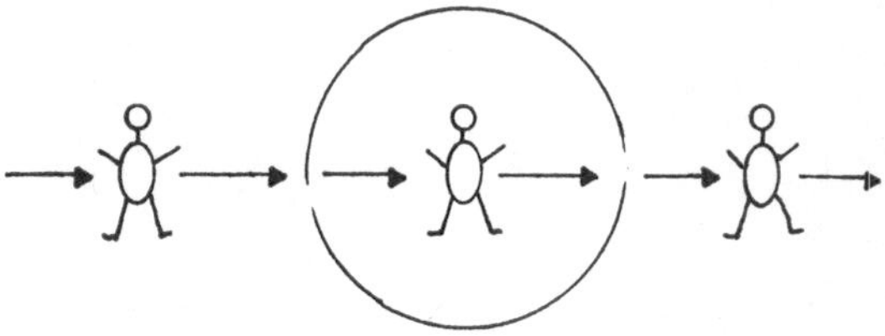

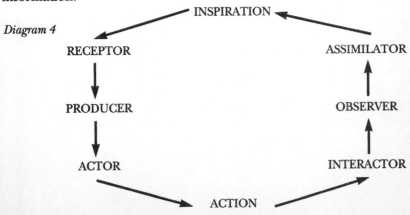

They believe that they are just innocent pawns in the game of chance called Life. They are unable or unwilling to see that it is their thoughts which create the world which they perceive. If they want to change painful or destructive patterns of a lifetime they need to become more conscious of their thoughts, sending out only those which produce healthier and happier results.

As you see, we play many roles in life; often simultaneously. We are the receptor of the inspiration, the producer of the thoughts, the actors and the interactors, the observer of our own life story and the assimilator of the information.

Diagram 4

INSPIRATION

RECEPTOR → PRODUCER → ACTOR → ACTION → INTERACTOR → OBSERVER → ASSIMILATOR

All roles are essential for our evolution and none is more important than the other. Each is attached to a higher wisdom and each role is susceptible to an illusion which can create stagnation and prevent soul growth.

It is only by tuning into our intuition or inner guidance that we can be certain that our thoughts and actions resonate with our deep inner truth, steering a clear course between the rocks of illusion and the eddies of stagnation.

The mirror of life always reflects reality. It is we who wear the "blinkers" seeing only what we want to see or allowing outdated belief systems to guide us.

As the Taoist teacher Lin Ching-hsi said:

> *"A mirror will reflect all things perfectly whether they are beautiful or ugly: it never refuses to show a thing, nor does it retain the thing after it is gone. The mind should be as open as this".*

I believe that the purpose of life is to experience wholeness and thereby express the Light of our soul in its entirety. Since the word *healing* means to *make whole* we would also reflect total health.

I also believe that the blueprint for wholeness is already present within our energetic memory and that all we have to do is to uncover those parts of ourselves which are still hidden and reconnect them to the core of our being.

And why did they become separate in the first place? Well, my understanding is that when we chose to inhabit this world and adopt the physical form with its emotions, instincts, etc. certain aspects of our being became masked and disappeared into the shadows. But the beauty is that this was all part of the Greater Plan.

In the process of re-connection we have the opportunity to employ our creative energies in a way which will not only benefit ourselves but which will also add to the Universal experience.

Unfortunately, many have forgotten their purpose and have become transfixed by the masks rather than by what they cover, misusing their creative energies to reinforce these illusions.

I believe, however, that the inspiring force which motivates us towards wholeness is still present in every individual and that this force is represented in physical form by the very breath which keeps us alive. As we breathe in we are subconsciously inspired to reach for wholeness, so that 18 times per minute we are reminded of our contract with the Creator.

And if there is an urge guiding us towards re-connection and wholeness then this means that we already possess the inner knowing that such connection is not just possible but already exists on some level.

*We cannot search for something unless we already know
of its existence.
We cannot dream of happiness, peace of mind or contentment
unless we already know that the dream can become a reality.*

Analogy

The picture of a completed jigsaw puzzle is shown on the lid of the box, but the pieces within the box are still separate and need to be joined in order to reflect the original picture.

The enjoyment of the puzzle comes from examining, experimenting and discovering how the pieces fit together, culminating in the final satisfaction of success.

We create our own reality so that we may experience wholeness.

By entering the mirror of existence we attract towards us people, situations, objects and events which in some way reflect those aspects which are still masked or separate. Through our interaction with these people and experiences, we are able to acknowledge and accept those parts, integrating them within our being so that we may become whole and healed. (Diagram 5)

Diagram 5

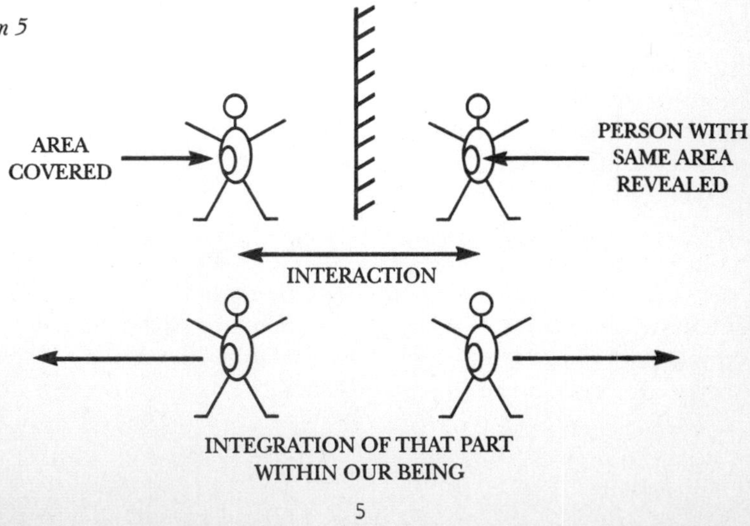

AREA COVERED →

PERSON WITH SAME AREA REVEALED

← INTERACTION →

INTEGRATION OF THAT PART
WITHIN OUR BEING

5

When the correct connection is made there is a sense of harmony and we move on to the next piece which is unattached. However, occasionally, as with a jigsaw puzzle, we try to force two pieces together which are ill-matched and cause disharmony or disease.

The higher wisdom suggests that we dismantle those pieces and try again. But on many occasions we ignore the feelings and even attempt to build around the defective image in order to satisfy our deception. All future efforts are then directed towards an illusion until we acknowledge the wisdom to start afresh.

Example:

I apply for a new job and, although I have reservations that my qualifications do not entirely match the job description, when I am offered the post, I accept gratefully.

At first, I work hard to do what is expected of me despite feeling the strain of working in an unknown field. I even take extra tuition in order to cope but find that, as the weeks go by, I am having to do more and more overtime to keep up.

Eventually, I become sick and cannot work for several weeks. During this time I realise that my intuition had advised me not to take the post but I had failed to listen; instead I had tried to build on the illusion that I could manage. I hand in my notice and look for a job more suited to my skills.

Only when we have the courage to accept our mistakes and learn by them, do we start to grow.

Life offers continuous opportunities for expansion. We can, of course, choose to walk around with our eyes closed, our ears blocked and our head down. Or we can start to realise the tremendous potential for growth which is staring us in the face if we only have the courage to open ourselves to life and stop searching for an easy escape.

More people fear life than they do death!

Some hope to grow just by reading books, attending seminars or by asking the opinion of others. But in the end we need to have the commitment to reveal, examine, experience and release episodes in our chosen life which we have created in order to enhance the Light emerging from our inner core.

The purpose of life is not to gain intellectual knowledge but to experience that knowledge. It is only through our total participation in the event that we attain wholeness and we cannot achieve this from the sidelines.

However much we may wish to avoid emotional involvement by standing on the outside with our books and acquired knowledge, life has a wonderful way of dragging us in.

Just when you thought you were safely detached from the problems which beset human beings, you are drawn into the physical world through trauma, illness, family commitments or essential work involvement.

We are here to live life and that sometimes means getting our hands dirty, our feet wet and recognising the beauty of imperfection.

This book explores the levels of consciousness or awareness which are the power behind the creation of our reality.

In other words:

If we are instinctual beings then survival is paramount.

If our emotions control us then we will attract emotional situations.

If logic rules then structure and objectivity are important.

If intuition guides us then we are in touch with our Inner Being.

The images reflected in the mirror will always reveal the dominant level of consciousness from which we act although we may not always wish to redress any imbalance. Instead we may lose ourselves in the illusions believing that there is no other way.

Much of what I write is based on reflections gathered over a lifetime's interest and involvement in the healing arts and as an observer of life through my work as a doctor and teacher within both orthodox and complementary fields.

I also include personal reflections for those traits which I have observed in others must surely be a reflection of my own inner blueprint.

If I see three consecutive patients with the same problem and provide some "wonderful" advice, I need to listen. For those whom I attract towards me for healing, will also be my healers.

Anything which holds our attention for more than a few minutes, including our work or hobbies, will always reflect an aspect of ourselves which desires to become whole.

When I function as a doctor, I am working on my need for healing.

When I'm teaching, I need to learn.
If you work with those who have no permanent home:
    where are you homeless or insecure?
If you work with those who have been abused:
    which part of you is being abused or misused?
If you work with communication:
    with whom do you wish to communicate?
If you love to travel:
    are you expanding your horizons or escaping?
If you are a carer:
    do you care for yourself as much as you care for others?

Our occupation, hobbies and interests mirror part of ourselves. It is wonderful to be dedicated to your work but, if you really wish to perform to the best of your ability, first recognise what the job is showing you and integrate that aspect within yourself. Then you will be successful in all you do.

Of course, there is the chance that following the integration you will no longer have a need to stay in that position and it will then be time to move on to another reflected image of your inner life.

I have met a number of women who were abused in their childhood and who by conscious or subconscious design worked with those who had also been abused. However, after much personal therapy and inner searching, they reached a stage when they wished to place that episode of their life behind them and realised that they were then ready to find a new occupation.

Another part of my work, as with all therapists and teachers, is to become a clear reflector for the patients and participants of Workshops. In order to do this it is important that I maintain a clean mirror which is not smudged by my own unfinished business or unresolved issues.

Therefore I am constantly aware of the need to allow into my consciousness only that which works from the Light for the good of all concerned and to dissolve away old patterns of existence which are no longer appropriate.

I also remember that when I am teaching there is in fact nothing new to teach and that all that I am doing is to remind people of what they already know. My only responsibility is to create a loving, vibrational environment which allows others to resonate with their own inner truth.

Any healer . . .
is only as good as his ability to heal himself.
Any teacher . . .
can only teach that which he already inwardly knows.

And why write the book now?

I believe that despite the tremendous strides which have taken place on this planet over the past decade, in terms of expanding our awareness to global problems, another "wake-up call" is required to help us to open our eyes to our own immediate areas of concern.

The easiest way to achieve this is to realign our hearts with our higher wisdom so that we can receive the increased vibration of Light which is now entering our inner and outer atmospheres.

The Light enables us to see our true path and purpose. But in order that we may be free to walk along that path, the Light will also illuminate parts of ourselves which have languished for too long in the shadows and which need to be integrated into our total being.

We are being presented with exciting new challenges which require us to step into unknown territory but which will allow us to reach our full potential as spiritual human beings, creating lives which are far more harmonious and inspiring than we have ever experienced before.

The "wake-up call" is for everybody but the final decision is always with the individual.

No-one can or will make the choice for you.

This is a time for letting go of old patterns of behaviour and transforming our desires into those which are beneficial for the Universe and not just for the individual. For too long we have been driven by our own personal needs whether openly or subtly mainly because we had forgotten that there was another way. This has created power struggles or "games" which further separated us from our own truth and from other people.

The planet has also suffered over the years with little concern being shown for its well-being with the focus of attention being directed towards our own immediate needs.

We need to consider the legacy that we are leaving behind. Money, people, jobs and material goods have a very short shelf-life. The water, the air, the earth and the sun will continue long after we have gone.

Honour and respect Mother Earth for the gifts she provides unconditionally.

Whether you have children or not, what values do you wish to pass down to the young people of the world so that they can live harmonious and full lives?

What would you write in a letter to inspire and encourage a new-born infant?

How could you change your life from today onwards so that it becomes more fulfilling and nurturing?

These values are the only aspects of inheritance which really matter and which will withstand the winds of change.

It is time to step into our lives and take control, reconnecting with our spiritual roots so that we can release the need to play games and start to live life freely knowing that there is no beginning and no end but just a continuum of consciousness.

My aim throughout this book is to keep the story of life simple for I believe that essentially it is. It is through man's use of words that it has become so complex. The gift of language was given to us so that we might communicate a greater range of impressions and, hence, grow.

However, for generations long words have been used to impress a few people whilst the majority were kept in the dark. Instead of using language to express a thought, too often words have succeeded in suffocating it.

I shall attempt to remove some of the barriers surrounding our thoughts without weakening the structure for I believe that with a little more light and air an idea will be able to start breathing on its own.

Keep it simple and we can all share the knowledge.

There is one essential truth which I hope will inspire you to come further with me on this path of discovery.

Despite living in a three-dimensional world we are, in fact, multi-dimensional beings, unlimited by time and space. There is only one time and that is . . . **NOW!**

Forget your belief in past lives and after lives and enjoy life fully in the present moment. For what you think, feel, say and do now generates the creative energy and inspiration which will fuel any future (or past) plans.

Choosing to live consciously in the moment requires us to focus our chaotic and often distracting thoughts so that they do not become the driving force which moulds our future.

So often we become obsessed by "the dirty mark on the carpet" failing to notice the beauty and splendour of the rest of the floor covering. We spend years examining those parts of our personality which are inadequate rather than recognising that they represent only a tiny percentage of who we are. By living in our own multi-dimensional light we gain perspective and the spot on the carpet can be transformed with ease.

It is also important to acknowledge that this beautiful planet Earth represents just one aspect of the Mother consciousness and that it is the present habitation of our soul. Let us move away from the idea that we are only here temporarily and that soon we will ascend to a better place where the angels sing and where we will receive our rewards for good deeds.

This is it!

The angels are singing now if only we would stop to listen. The gifts are abundant if only we would stop seeking approval from a higher authority and start to give without expectations. Learning to receive gracefully without the fear of losing oneself in the action is also part of the rhythm of life.

We can only connect fully and intimately with others when we know who we are; and we can only know who we are by connecting fully and intimately with others.

Without this connection to our inner self, to others or to the Source we often experience pain and fear, both of which are telling us that some part of ourselves has become separated and that we need to start the re-connection.

Unfortunately, in many cases these messengers become the enemy leading to a sense of helplessness, chaos and confusion causing us to panic and give our power to someone else so that we can experience a false sense of security.

Only when we see pain and fear in the right perspective can we take control of our own life, asking for help in a positive manner and hence start the process of reconciliation.

Fear of change often inhibits the expansion towards wholeness allowing limited thoughts and expectations to control us. We then mirror these thoughts in the outside world and attract towards us people and situations which we then use as an excuse for our failure to change.

> *External conditions and other people cannot prevent us reaching wholeness and expressing our Inner Light unless on some level they do so with our blessing.*

It is time to recognise that some of the limiting states are in fact illusions which are no longer applicable to the present situation.

"*I'm not limited*", I hear you say. "*I'm a free agent*".

Are you?

Listen to yourself.

Listen to the controlling words and thoughts in your vocabulary "I should/must/ought/can't/won't" or the excuses: "too busy, too poor, too tired" or the eternal: "It's not that easy!"

Which belief system limits you?

Recently I was listening to a story about a man who had suffered a heart attack; after twenty minutes the pupils of his eyes were fixed and dilated and he had no pulse. Following medical protocol that these signs denote extinction of physical life, the doctor present proclaimed him dead.

However, a friend of the man, ignorant of medical knowledge and untouched by years of medical experience, refused to accept the diagnosis and continued to apply resuscitation techniques despite the scepticism of the doctor.

Two hours later the patient woke up and wondered where he was.

This story reached deep within my soul and I felt confused. Through my esoteric training I know that miracles happen. However, when wearing my medical hat, I agreed with the doctor, finding it difficult to see beyond the confines of my experience and scientific training.

I realised that where my spiritual views were in conflict with deeply entrenched orthodox training, my actions as a carer could be subtly influenced. Neither belief system is right or wrong but the awareness of conflict allowed me to find a point of harmony within.

What limits you?

Most of us hold on to outdated thoughts as their presence makes us believe that we are in control. In truth, if we fear losing that control, then we never had it in the first place. Only when we have the courage to let go do we gain control – but this time the control comes from an inner sense of knowing.

If you are dissatisfied with your life then you have the free-will to change it; this is the one certainty on this planet. We have been given the gift of free-will or choice.

Use it wisely, with love and understanding. So many people only demand choice when they are threatened that it may be taken away, such as when a decision needs to be made on a course of treatment.

"I don't want someone to tell me what to do" (but I do want someone else to make the final decision!)

Most people have never exercised their right of free-will (or choice) and happily give their power away to others in order to avoid taking responsibility for their own existence. Hence they have never had to accept that the path to wholeness consists of many wrong turnings.

If we accept the challenge of life . . . mistakes are inevitable but rarely fatal.

I only have to look at my own profession to see how defensive medicine has now become in response to the fear of being sued.

Helplessness is rife whilst spontaneity and individual expression are discouraged.

Where is the power? Where is the free-will? So often it has become buried beneath a history of strife, oppression and bureaucracy reinforced by the use of weapons, the power of money and through manipulation of the mind.

It is time to re-connect to your own inner truth and start to express it in a way which honours and respects all those who live within this beautiful planet, Earth.

One of our greatest allies in helping us to move towards this point of centredness is our physical body which through illness reveals both the need for change as well as the direction.

Throughout this book I will reveal my own understanding of the message of disease in relation to our desire to become whole.

I share my thoughts with you as I too seek ways in which I can stand in my own Light for I believe that continual questioning, searching and discovery are the way of the scientist.

Recently, I was challenged by a fellow doctor who asked:

"How can you, with all your scientific training, believe all this?"

I replied, "How can you with all your scientific training stand by and watch people become sick and die and never question what more could be done?"

I have no desire to create new dogmas, ideals or illusions. Those days are finished. All the knowledge you need is already present somewhere within your own consciousness waiting to be brought into the light. I offer you some of my thoughts which I hope will resonate with your own truth thus enabling the process of enlightenment.

So . . . are you willing to come with me on a journey of discovery?

I will be your guide and provide the Light. All you need to bring with you is an open mind, a loving heart and the willingness to become the beautiful spiritual human being that, in essence, you already are.

Chapter 2

From Inspiration To Action

To be able to understand the mirror of our existence and how we create our own reality we need to find the original creative spark and watch it pass through the various stages of evolution before it emerges as action.

For man this process takes place largely in the mind which contrary to common belief is not limited to the brain. In fact, the mind involves many different levels of consciousness which span the dimensions from Universal Intelligence to that of the cell nucleus.

It is now well-known that there is very active communication between the various cells of the body which respond to our every thought and mood often without direct reference to the brain.

At any one moment we may be totally absorbed in our daily activities but at the same time our mind is tapping into and processing information which it is receiving from extensive sources of intelligence within our world of existence.

Indeed it could be said that human beings are pure consciousness comprising of different aspects of intelligent activity which interact with one another to create what we know as a physical individual. (Diagram 6)

Diagram 6

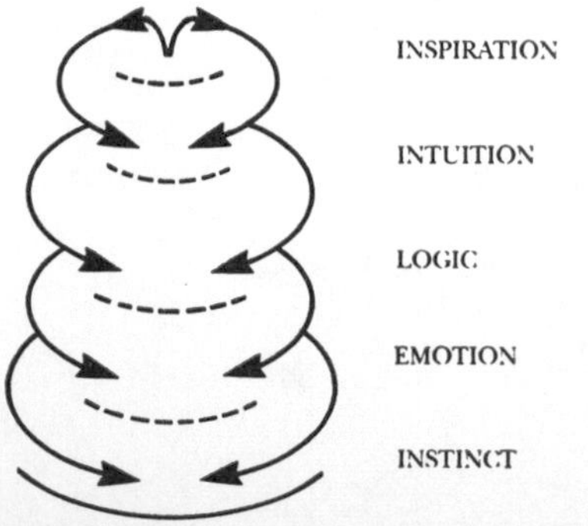

LEVELS OF
CONSCIOUSNESS

INSPIRATION

INTUITION

LOGIC

EMOTION

INSTINCT

Because our mind can access and inform varying levels of consciousness, it can be seen that every thought we have travels the airways influencing not only our own lives, but the evolution of other people, our planet, the solar system and even the Universe.

> *Thoughts are powerful creators of our reality,*
> *shaping the future existence of our planet;*
> *. . . . . use them wisely.*

They are far more influential than any words or actions for thoughts carry the intent. Remember an occasion when you spoke with a smiling face whilst at the same time felt angry and hurt. Or another time when your mind said "No" whilst your mouth said "Yes".

Despite your precautions the listener still picked up the negative vibrations subconsciously and may have come to distrust the words you speak. At the same time, your own inner being became confused receiving no clear indication as to the direction you wished to take.

Until we stop talking with "forked tongue" and start to be compassionately honest with ourselves and then others, the ability to trust will always be one of the greatest issues of mankind.

In *Mutant Message Down Under,* in which *Marlo Morgan* relates her time with the Aborigines, she asks why it is that they are able to communicate via mental telepathy whilst most people of industralised countries have forgotten the art.

Their answer is simple; the gift became buried with our need to keep secrets from each other for we believed it was only through secrets that we could maintain our individual identity.

Are you ready to let others read your mind?

And, if not, are you willing to start to live life believing they can?

If we want to bring peace and harmony to our planet, respecting and honouring every individual for their uniqueness, we first have to clear the pollution of our thoughts. And we can only do this when we feel secure in who we are and honour our birthright.

As we follow the path of creation, I hope that it will become clear as to the way forward and the means by which we can start to move beyond the obstacles which prevent us from being true to ourselves.

The creative process taking place in the mind follows various steps and can be summarised as:

I am inspired with an idea from Universal consciousness
I focus my intention to create through my intuition
I produce a thought-form through the application of logic
I provide colour and movement to the thought by mobilising the emotions
I express and release the action into the physical world

Now imagine that the physical world is not only the location where the action occurs but is also a mirror which relays back to you the result of your thought processes.

Then as an observer you are able to reflect upon your action through the following process:

I instinctively examine the survival of the creation
I react to the expression of the action through feelings
I focus the feelings using logic to create a belief system
I check intuitively that the belief system resonates with my inner truth
I release the reaction so that it can be the seed for the next inspiration

Diagram 7

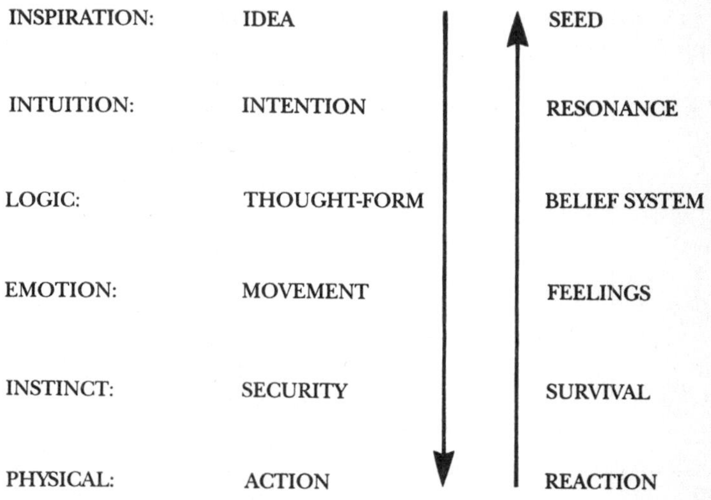

INSPIRATION:	**IDEA**		**SEED**
INTUITION:	**INTENTION**		**RESONANCE**
LOGIC:	**THOUGHT-FORM**		**BELIEF SYSTEM**
EMOTION:	**MOVEMENT**		**FEELINGS**
INSTINCT:	**SECURITY**		**SURVIVAL**
PHYSICAL:	**ACTION**		**REACTION**

We need all the aspects of our mind to be able to function fully as a spiritual human being. This means that our emotions and instincts are just as important as our intuition. However, through evolution it was not uncommon for one stage of this process to become dominant whilst others were blocked, restricted or even omitted.

We are presently in the *fifth root race* of man's development on the Earth. Little is known of the first two races which occurred millions of years ago but as we study the expansion of human consciousness we are also tracking human evolution.

The chapters which follow provide an understanding of the mind and the means by which the various elements can work in harmony.

Within the text there will be references to the energy centres or *chakras* which are found throughout the body although I will be concentrating on the main chakras which run from the top of the head to the base of the spine (Diagram 8).

The purpose of these centres is to integrate the energy which is emitted from the various levels of consciousness and focus it directly into the physical body.

In this way, our actions and bodily functions are almost totally dependent on the activity of our mind.

During evolution specific chakras have been particularly sensitive to the circulating energies and some of this residual influence is still affecting us at this time.

So, as we work to create a clear channel for the incoming impulses by clearing our mind of unnecessary thoughts, we also recreate harmony within these energy centres so that nothing can prevent us emitting our true Light.

Diagram 8

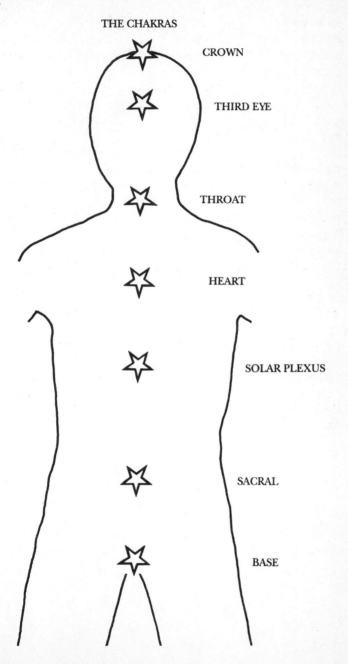

THE CHAKRAS

CROWN

THIRD EYE

THROAT

HEART

SOLAR PLEXUS

SACRAL

BASE

Chapter 3

Inspiration
The Breath of Life

"Eureka" shouted Archimedes as he jumped from the bath having been inspired to understand the principle behind the measurement of density. An apple falling on Newton's head inspired him, providing science with the Law of Gravitation.

Both men allowed the focus of their minds to move beyond what was known at that time and be open to new concepts which the world needed.

Most of us will not reach the dizzy heights of these great pioneers in terms of inspiration but we have all, at some time in our lives, moved beyond logic and said "Yee-s-s" to life.

We may have been inspired to call someone, clear out cupboards, visit an old friend, fly to the Bahamas, volunteer to work in India, apply for a new job or to ask the man or woman of our dreams to marry us.

Each time, we took a deep breath and stepped into a new dimension of thought, emotion and action.

So what is inspiration?

The word comes from the Latin *spirare* which means to breathe and represents not only the in-breath but also "a thought of divine or supernatural influence".

To be inspired is to be animated by an idea or impulse leading to action or the creation of something which had not been seen in this particular form before and may not be linked to previous personal experience.

"I just did it. Why? I was inspired and knew that everything would be alright".

Such divine thought is linked to the Breath of God which gives life to all that exists within the Universe. This same breath animates the foetus during the act of conception. It then inspires the newborn child to release its dependence on the mother's life-force and to take its first breath in order that the indwelling soul can start its journey upon the earth.

And it doesn't stop there; for on each in-breath we are born renewed, inspired to be co-creators of this beautiful planet. On the out-breath, we die into the moment, releasing into the environment our gift of life, knowing that as day follows night, we will once again be inspired by this sacred energy.

How we use this source of power is totally dependent on our openness to the incoming impulse and the realisation that the act of breathing is far more than just moving gases in and out.

For too long, people have relied on pills, alcohol and drugs in order to increase the excitement in their lives rather than turning to their own natural resources.

As the ancient sages knew:

As we breathe, we think and as we think, we are!

Many people would recognise the truth of this statement for, when we are tense, calming of the mind and body occurs by taking long deep breaths. Similarly, when we are depressed, increasing our rate of respiration stimulates the nervous system with noticeable changes in the motivation and enthusiasm we then direct towards our activities.

So from the first breath to the last, we have the opportunity to link with the most powerful source of creation in the Universe and start to build the world as we would want it to be.

Without this knowledge we are purely puppets in the game of life breathing to stay alive rather than being "breathed" by life.

Just imagine how you would feel if on each in-breath you experienced emotions such as happiness, peace of mind, excitement, inner tranquillity or a real sense of belonging.

And then imagine the impact of that out-breath on your activities and on those around you.

The realisation of your dreams is but a breath away.

Inspiration is also connected to enlightenment for as we are inspired we are filled with Light which reveals something which until then was hidden. In this way we become aware of our true potential and then make space for spirit to take form.

Phrases within our language confirm this hypothesis:

"I saw the Light"
"Suddenly the Light dawned"
"I could see things more clearly"
"It suddenly dawned on me"

With each in-breath, we create a vacuum within ourselves which, on a physical level, draws in air. At the same time our spiritual body attracts Light, filling us with exciting new ideas.

On the out-breath, as we release the carbon dioxide, we also express these animated visions and thoughts into the world. This is the process of creation.

Diagram 9

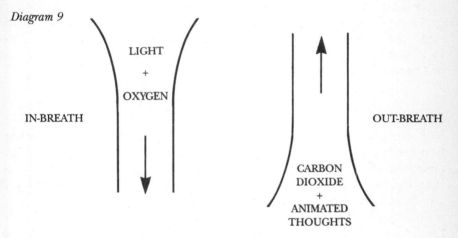

LIGHT
+
OXYGEN

IN-BREATH

OUT-BREATH

CARBON
DIOXIDE
+
ANIMATED
THOUGHTS

The incoming oxygen can be seen as a reflection of the Light's life giving energy and is essential to the survival of each cell of the body. The expired carbon dioxide is a reflection of expressed animated form, consisting of carbon which is the basic component of all physical life, combined with the inspiring oxygen.

And yet one of the most inspiring moments of the whole breathing cycle is the pause between the out-breath and the next in-breath for it is:
- *within this silence that we are closest to the Source of Light*
- *within this pause that we relinquish our will to the Will of our Creator*
- *within this moment that we enter timelessness and unlimited dimensions of space where we re-connect fully to our spiritual nature*

Until we are willing to give ourselves time to enter that space of nothingness and stillness, we can never know the vastness of eternity, the strength of surrender and the peace which comes with re-connection.

Learning the art of correct breathing and maintaining the practice every day can greatly change physical and mental health and help us to become increasingly focused on the purpose of our life.

I believe that breath training, as used in many yogic practices, should be an essential part of any therapy, be it complementary or orthodox. In this way, the patient becomes an active participant in their own healing process, through inspiration, release and re-connection.

Now to take the link between thought and breath to a further stage. Imagine that it is not only through our nose and mouth that we breathe but that we can also draw Light into our body through the energy centre at the top of our head, called the crown chakra.

This centre is one of the major ways in which the higher levels of intelligence enter our brain and body and can be likened to the blow-hole on top of the head of a dolphin and a whale.

So, to become inspired not only with air but also with higher wisdom, one should imagine drawing the Light in through the crown chakra on each in-breath and passing it around the body on expiration.

Diagram 10

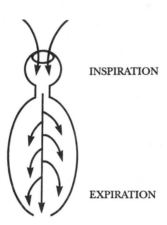

INSPIRATION

EXPIRATION

This chakra is directly linked to the **pineal gland** which is now being recognised by the medical profession as an important link between health and illness.

We know that it is stimulated by the electro-magnetic forces of the sun and helps us to find our direction in life and that imbalances within the gland appear to be connected to diseases such as depression, schizophrenia and SAD (seasonal affective disorder).

The gland is thought to be of a crystalline nature amplifying energies which pass through it. There is evidence that in this way breath allied with sound, focused at the pineal gland, actually increases the light vibration within the subtle bodies of the individual leading to a greater sense of well-being.

More research is needed in this area but I believe that sound, light and trained breathing are the medicines of tomorrow.

An inspired idea is rarely personal at its inception and acts merely as a creative spark to stimulate our minds into activity. If we wish to experience our own "Eureka" we need to be willing to move beyond personal needs and problems and to activate the higher realms of consciousness.

At that level we may find that a number of people have received the same idea in different parts of the world at the same time. On each occasion the insight appears to reach conscious awareness almost out of the blue and may be unrelated to present day thinking.

It is then a race against time to see who will be the first person to patent this apparently unique idea!

(I believe that by allowing several people to receive the same message our Creator was hedging his/her bets, hoping that at least one person would carry the message through to the end!)

To complete the connection with breathing, we would all acknowledge that the air which we inhale now has passed through many sets of lungs before reaching us, involving people from different parts of the world and from different periods of time.

In the same way, it can be seen that inspirational thought is probably also not new but, because of time and space changes, will be approached in a different manner as if it were fresh. Any animating idea therefore will have been through several minds before reaching this point of evolution.

This makes we wonder whose mind has previously been the vehicle for the thoughts which I now write in this book!

EXERCISES FOR INSPIRATION

To become fully open to inspiration we first need to learn to breathe with awareness. Here are a few exercises to encourage this attitude:

1) Easy Breathing

Sit or lie comfortably. On the in-breath, expand your chest and abdomen drawing air into this increased space through your nose and the top of your head.

On the out-breath, with an audible sigh, fully release, moving the air out through the mouth and the top of the head, squeezing out the last drop by tightening the abdominal muscles.

Use the count of six in and eight out, with a pause of three after the out-breath. Treasure the stillness and serenity which exists within the pause, allowing the time to lengthen with practice.

2) Spreading the Light

Imagine that on each in-breath, you are drawing in light through the top of the head following the procedure given above. You can add colour to the light especially purple, violet, white and gold for these are more commonly associated with higher inspiration.

On the out-breath, send the light out to all areas of your body, starting with the tips of your fingers and toes, then to the top of your head and then to the organs and cells.

Repeat this on several breaths using the count of six in and eight out, with a pause of three after the out-breath. You may find that the body starts to tingle, which is good. If this occurs, you may wish to send the excess Light from your body into the ether, into Mother Earth or to those you love.

This exercise allows you to become energised with pure light, opening your heart and mind to your own higher wisdom and inspiration.

3) Breathing to Energize

If you are feeling tired or low, use the same breathing techniques described above but increase the count to four in and four out, breathing in and out through the nose and top of head. Remember to pause again after the out-breath, this time for the count of two.

Straighten your posture with the in-breath, drawing the air into every part of your body and anchoring it into the ground. On the out-breath let this vital energy clear away old emotional blockages leaving you with a sense of strength and vitality.

Within the pause, acknowledge the constant stream of energy which is available to you when you surrender to the truth of your existence.

4) Breathing to Calm Yourself

When you are feeling anxious or stressed, slow the pace of breathing to four in and eight out, with a pause of three at the end of the out-breath. Let the body and mind relax fully with each out-breath, surrendering to the chair, bed or floor and allowing it to support you.

If you are seated, you may wish to bend forward on the out-breath and return to an upright position on the in-breath, as if you were being rocked, but don't forget the pause.

To become more conscious of inspirational thoughts, I suggest the following:

a) Enhancing Inspiration

Send out a message as you wake, before meditation and before you go to sleep that you are ready and open to be inspired for the purpose of inner learning and to be of service to the Universe.

b) Record Inspirational Thoughts

Keep a notebook close to you and jot down any thoughts or ideas which appear to be disassociated with present day situations and which are not necessarily linked to personal desires.

Remember the initial idea may be quite vague at first and it is important to ask your higher self for more information or guidance. If nothing comes initially, let the idea stay in the notebook and just check it every few weeks to see whether related thoughts have appeared which can help you to take this impulse further.

c) Thought into Action

Have the courage to act on these inspirational thoughts for they are truly a gift from God. Use your intuition to guide you, your logic to focus the ideas, your emotions to move them and your instincts to ensure their survival and then . . . . just let go and allow the Universe to do the rest!

Chapter 4

Intuition
An Inner Knowing

The power of the intuition is still in its infancy with most individuals on this planet relying extensively upon their logic, emotions and instincts to meet their personal needs. And yet as the 21st Century approaches, it is emerging as the most important function of the mind bringing greater compassion, peace and unity to our world.

It is related to the right brain activity with its creative bias and is often seen as a woman's prerogative defined as "illogical logic". And yet throughout our history those with such insight and wisdom have been revered for their talents.

Most of the greatest entrepreneurs of today excel because they have the courage and determination to follow an intuitive hunch. At first they may receive scorn and derision from their colleagues who prefer to commit to an idea only when it has been fully investigated and when all risks have been removed.

However, the smiles soon recede when success is showered upon "the risk-taker".

There are many successful partnerships whether in marriage or business which rely on one partner being intuitive while the other is practical, ensuring that the inspired idea becomes manifest.

Intuition is far more personal than inspiration and yet still universally objective, reflecting that what is beneficial for the individual will, on a soul level, benefit all concerned.

When we act intuitively we can never work in isolation for intuition touches the heart and mind of everyone we encounter.

Intuition embraces the creative flash adding intention to this inspirational idea with the aim of moving it towards physical activity. Untouched by the limitation of the three-dimensional world, the question posed by the higher mind can be:

"What do I need to reach my greatest potential?"
Rather than:
"What is available to me?"

The force and scope of creation is unlimited.
It is the narrow perception of ourselves which creates the limitation.

Intuition also provides an overview to the emotional reactions we experience in response to life situations, helping us to gain a clearer perspective on what appears to be a chance occurrence.

Diagram 11

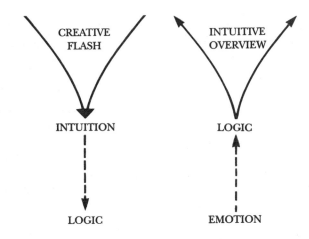

Ask most people when they use their intuition and they will give answers such as:
- *when I meet people for the first time*
- *when I am viewing a house with the intention of buying*
- *when I am deciding where to sit in a train compartment*
- *when there is a major decision to be made*

These replies are just the tip of the iceberg in terms of the possible widespread application of intuition in our lives. When we are working from our intuition we will combine the information from our instincts, our emotions and from our logic and formulate a decision from a non-judgemental point of view using wisdom and compassion.

We will look beyond the initial reaction and ask ourselves questions such as:
"What can I learn from this experience?"

"What do I need to change in order to feel better about this situation?"
"What can I say in order to clear the air?"
"How can I help others to know what I am feeling?"

However, too often we confuse our intuition with "gut feelings" finding ourselves purely reacting without ever taking the response to a higher level of understanding.

Gut feelings emerge from the energy centre known as the solar plexus; its purpose is to help us achieve self-worth and self-value. But, if this centre is acting alone, it will aim to maintain our own personal power at the expense of others, leading to increased sensitivity and wariness towards our environment and those who live within it.

We then see the world outside as the problem and are unwilling to look at our own part in the drama especially if it involves taking responsibility for our thoughts and actions.

We enter each new situation with a subconscious bag of pre-conceived ideas concerning people and life, based on previous experience, associated emotions and the social or cultural training which we received in our formative years.

Any encounter is then matched against these criteria with minimal space for diversity. In this way we miss the chance to really appreciate the individual behind the outward appearance.

And, because everybody we meet is reflecting some part of ourselves, we also miss the opportunity to find out who we really are.

Don't judge a book by its cover!
Don't judge your fellow travellers on this Earth by their appearance!

Without the gift of intuition your initial perception or understanding may well be flawed or deficient!

At this time in our history when society, supported by the media, is telling us to trust nobody, the solar plexus is working overtime often creating excessive reactions to non-life threatening situations. I believe that on a physical level this heightened hypersensitivity is partly responsible for the increase in illnesses due to allergies, such as asthma and eczema.

Unless we wish to create a far greater fear-based society, it is time that we brought some rationale and wisdom back into this equation. The way forward is to allow the intuition to guide us towards a better life where there is trust, generosity of spirit and the ability to know what is best for the individual soul without the need to judge others.

Learning to trust ourselves through the power of love, enables us to trust others with the same generosity.

Example:

You enter an almost empty restaurant and see an old man sitting at one of the tables. He appears unclean, untidy and looks miserable. You decide to go and sit at a table on the other side of the room.

As you eat your meal, he starts a conversation. At first you try to avoid him but eventually you look up and see this most lively and compassionate face staring back at you.

As the conversation continues you realise that behind this rather "battered" appearance is someone of great wisdom and humour gained through a lifetime of experience.

By the end of the meal you are sharing a table with your new "teacher" learning about humility and non-judgmental attitudes.

Look beyond the outer covering.
Where are your teachers?
They often appear in disguise waiting for the student to lift their eyes beyond their limited horizons.

There are times when intuition will guide us away from danger whether this is on a physical, spiritual or psychological level. The message then often appears without prior warning or expectation and provides us with information which is non-emotional and immediate:

"Get out of this situation **now**!"

Learning to trust intuition actually frees us from illusionary dangers and allows us to focus on the more pleasurable aspects of our world.

However, by listening to intuition, I cannot guarantee that you will avoid pain and suffering but hopefully such discomfort will be purely a means to an end and therefore short lived.

Indeed, on many occasions, the intuition will provide us with tests which we may not **want** but which on most occasions we **need**!

To achieve its objective the soul will use any method to bring into the light those areas of your being which are presently in darkness. It will provide you with challenges which may at first appear impossible and yet it knows that, by stretching you beyond your present limits, you will eventually reach within and find your own inner strength in order to expand your horizons.

Diagram 12

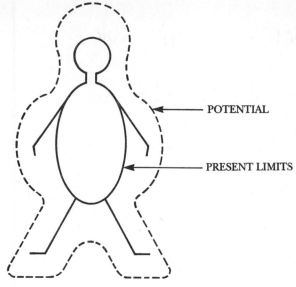

POTENTIAL

PRESENT LIMITS

It is only by listening to the intuition and learning to trust it that most of us will find the fulfilment we seek whether this is peace of mind, connection with others, unconditional love, success or inner contentment.

So let me provide further definitions of intuition so that you may recognise when you are using it.

Intuition, like inspiration, often surfaces "out of the blue" without associated feelings and without any obvious points of reference. It may appear in the mind as a complete picture or package of information and yet remains relatively nebulous in terms of time and space, rarely setting time limits or focusing on detail.

The source of intuition is the *Higher Self* which is the part of our being which is connected to the Creator, to Universal Energy and to our highest spiritual ideals. The difference between the Soul and the Higher Self is that the latter does not incarnate into the physical body but remains as a permanent connection between the Soul and its spiritual source (diagram 13).

When we receive intuitive thought, it touches a point deep within our being providing us with a sense of inner knowing much as an old friend would remind us of something we had forgotten.

Our response is often immediate and natural:

"Ah, yes. Of course!"

Diagram 13

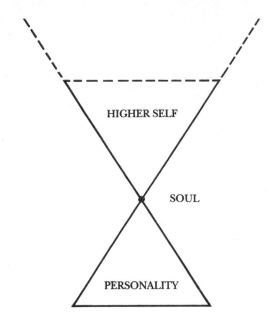

And when questioned about our desire to follow this feeling we often say:
"Don't ask me to explain or justify my reasons
I just know that this is the right direction"
Or "..... that I should do this thing"
Or "..... that this person is not right for me"

Our intuition is rarely wrong. More often it is our *analysis* of the message which is incomplete.

Don't try to understand or make sense of an intuitive impulse. Act upon it and then you will understand what it means!

It is often only in retrospect that we perceive with clarity why it was so important to follow our inner voice. Indeed we may find that our original understanding of the situation merely acted as an enticement to lure us towards the real reason for movement.

Analogy

You are invited to a party and although you are tired an inner urging persuades you to go.

After two hours, you wonder why on earth you agreed to come and decide to make tracks for home. As you go to collect your coat you meet an old friend whom you have not seen for a long time.

You decide to stay and spend a delightful evening together, at the end of which your friend offers you a job working in an area of interest which until then was only a dream.

On the way home you feel uplifted and whisper grateful thanks to your inner voice which always knows what is best for you.

Following your intuition is the path to soul fulfilment . . . . although the ultimate goal or purpose is often hidden at the commencement of the journey.

Diagram 14

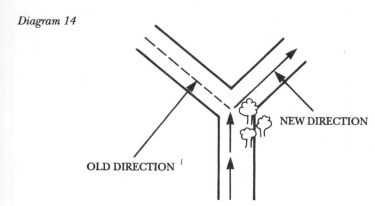

It is not uncommon to believe that we know our mission in life, only to find that on taking a few steps along our path, guided by the intuition, that a new vista has appeared, presenting us with totally different goals, aspirations and belief systems.

"A good traveller has no fixed plans and is not intent upon arriving.
A good artist lets his intuition lead him wherever it wants.
A good scientist has freed himself of concepts and keeps his mind open to what is."

(Tao Te Ching, Lao-tzu)

When we follow our intuition we need to be sensitive to new information which becomes available and be willing to make adjustments, however extreme, to our understanding of the purpose of our life.

There are no straight lines in Nature . . . be ready to go with the flow knowing that the ultimate directing force has only your best interests at heart.

Your intuition knows the type of incentive needed to attract your attention and to stimulate interest in such a way that you will, by your own accord, be motivated to follow the soul's message whilst still firmly believing that you are in total control of the situation.

For some individuals, such inducement involves the use of so-called "negative emotions" such as fear, anger or despair. These people believe that life is full of suffering and anxiety and tend to look for the most painful path whilst avoiding that which is easy and enjoyable.

Once their attention has been caught, they may actually be disconcerted by the message of the intuition, for it can appear unemotional and without the usual emotional blackmail.

"Believe in yourself". *"Go for it"*. *"Step back"*.

Others are driven by their passionate determination to achieve, compete or possess and tend to respond best to words such as *"should, ought, must"*. They too need to learn that the intuition is a friend who will neither praise nor criticise but which is always present.

Some people only listen to their intuition when they become ill. It is then that the conscious mind is less active and there is more time to focus on the needs of the soul, if they are willing to listen!

But the greatest and most powerful source of motivation is the desire to feel more joy, fun, love, fulfilment and happiness in one's life. For these emotions resonate with the energy of the intuition and can only strengthen the expression of our own inner truth.

The intuition knows our excuses, our "hang ups", our illusions about ourself and about the world and the games we play in order to stay in exactly the same miserable position!

"What about my job, family, husband?"

"It is easy for you to talk, I'm the one who is suffering".

"If I listen to my own needs, I would be seen as selfish".

"My partner would never understand". *(Have you asked them?)*

"Forget it. That is far too difficult".

"I'm trying to change". *(Trying is lying . . . Native American)*

"Yes but, what if . . . . . .".

And yet, like any loving parent, it loves us more because of these foibles and inconsistencies and uses humour and unconditional love to encourage the very best from its wayward child.

Now, where inspiration is linked to the lungs, intuition is linked to the heart. This is not so much the physical heart but its energetic counterpart, the heart chakra, which represents the eternal flame of our being, fanned by the incoming breath or inspiration.

This flame contains the promise of eternal life where there are no beginnings and no ends and where we are linked to all energetic forms in the Universe, as a multi-dimensional spiritual being.

Tuning into our intuition and following it faithfully allows us to stay connected to this truth as well as leading us towards the ultimate feeling of love and wholeness. When we disconnect from our intuition we often feel lost and separate and death becomes something to fear.

Following the intuition requires an open mind and heart.

Another way of relating the heart to the power of intuition is to imagine that the heart sounds a particular musical tone or note. This note resonates with the heart of our solar system, the Sun, and eventually with the heart of our Creator.

If our thoughts and actions harmonise with the tone within our own heart then we act in accordance with the needs of our inner self and of the Universe.

Diagram 15

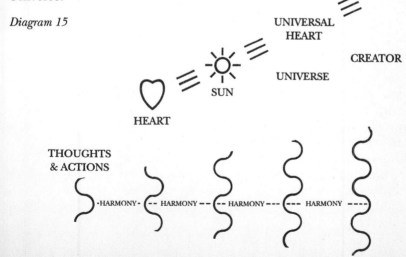

By following the Universal Law of Attraction, if we act from our intuition, energised by the power of love, we will attract towards us only that which brings the greatest benefit to all concerned, including ourselves.

When the intuition is active, we compare all advice, ideas and thoughts with the inner note of our heart. If they resonate, then we allow them to pass deeper into our consciousness; if they do not, then we should let them go.

Another area strongly connected to intuition is the energy centre called *the third eye* or *ajna* which is situated above the bridge of the nose, between the two physical eyes. This centre "focuses the intention to create" (*Alice Bailey: Esoteric Healing*) and provides clarity to the intuitive message.

The centre can be seen as the pivot around which creation occurs. This is because it is related to our outer world through the eyes, to the physical world via the pituitary and hypothalamus glands and to our inner energetic world through the crown and heart chakras.

Diagram 16

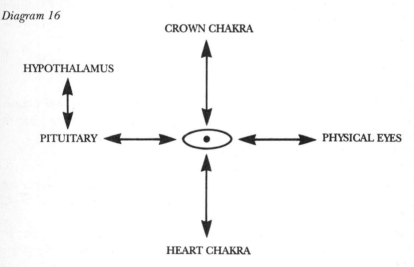

It receives inspiration from the crown and passes it to the heart in order to check whether there is resonance between the idea and the inner needs of the soul. It also matches the outgoing impulse with the manifested form within the outside world.

If there is disharmony between these two images, the individual will experience an imbalance within the third eye with the result that the energy from the crown and heart may well be ignored leaving the image from the outside world to direct our actions rather than any impulse from within.

Diagram 17

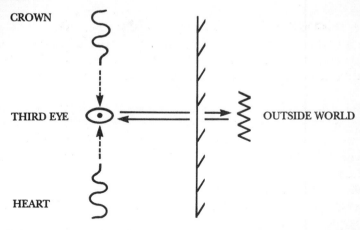

It is only by re-connecting the third eye to the crown and heart chakras that the balance is restored, with the higher self taking responsibility for creating reality through the power of intuition.

Intuitive impulses often enter our awareness during meditation, dream state or when the conscious mind is relaxed, for the soul knows that, left to their own devices, our logic or emotions will happily provide us with an answer without ever reaching to the seat of higher wisdom.

Logic or analysis says:

"I want this to be the truth and therefore I will block any intuitive thought which contradicts my desire and persuade myself that I know what is best for my life".

When the will is strong, then the higher self will send its messages at moments you least expect such as on first waking, whilst walking the dog, whilst relaxing or whilst cooking a meal.

The best way to be open to our intuition is to connect with our highest Light energy, clear our mind of pre-ordained responses and be willing to move with whatever advice is offered.

The source of the intuitive message may be outside our own thought processes. For instance, the words of another person can often act as an intuitive force mirroring our heart's desire.

"Why don't you do this?", they ask and somewhere inside this question resonates with you and you reply:

"Why not?"

Of course, there are other times when the truth is spoken and we don't necessarily want to hear!

It is always very comfortable to speak to those who provide you with excuses to stay in exactly the same position. But it is a true friend who sees intuitively what is needed and has the courage to share this information with you.

We usually know when the truth is being offered because it touches a raw nerve. If we are wise we will not turn our back on this informant but rather thank them for their loving support.

Sometimes we are the recipient of information about other people and then we have to use our intuition to decide whether this is the right time to share this knowledge.

Too often advice is blurted out at a most inopportune moment without the permission of the individual concerned, causing great distress.

The Native Americans say:
"Don't give advice unless asked for".

Some people receive insights which they believe should be shared with the general public in the name of spiritual enlightenment only to find on listening to their intuition that these insights are in fact purely for personal learning.

Whatever your intention, however noble, always listen to and follow the inner voice.

Even the media may be used to deliver an intuitive message although it is always important to check whether this reflects your inner values or whether you are listening to some clever subliminal message.

Remember to ask: *"Is this good for my soul growth or just for my ego?"*. If it is the latter forget it!

I remember being at a crossroads in my career, unsure of my next move. One day I was sitting flicking through a magazine which I had never read before and happened to see a small advertisement offering a job in a hospital abroad. I applied, was offered the post and ultimately that time in New Zealand turned my life around.

There may be occasions when you feel confused by the messages you are receiving. The way forward is to ask for greater clarity remembering that this may appear in a variety of ways often spiced with a sense of humour!

For instance you may switch on the radio or television and hear a programme discussing the very subject about which you were concerned. Or you may pick up a book and, on opening it randomly, find the answer you were looking for summed up in one sentence. Or you may find yourself following a van with a logo on the back whose message really strikes home.

I remember a time when life had become too serious and I felt as if I was carrying the world on my shoulders. I was sitting mulling over the problems of the day whilst waiting in a long line of traffic when suddenly I became aware of the van in front which was delivering lighting equipment to local shops.

On the back door, in very large letters was the statement:

"Lighten Up!"

I started to laugh and realised that things had to change. I turned the car around in the middle of the road and drove back home ready to allow some fun into my life again.

Some may say this is "just coincidence". Personally I don't believe that anything happens by chance but, if that is what you want to believe, that is fine.

However, I suspect you are missing some golden opportunities to enrich your life, for the more you follow these coincidences the more they occur, leading you always towards greater joy and soul fulfilment.

If you do ask for clarification or greater insight into a problem, please be receptive to the answer even though it may not be what you expected to hear and requires you to make changes in your life.

Some people need continuous reinforcement before they are willing to follow their intuition and this will be patiently provided. However, hopefully we will eventually move on the first occasion rather than waiting until the final push.

Another way of focusing your energy in the right direction is to use visualisation. I usually imagine a hallway along which there are many doors and ask that if there are areas in my life which are no longer appropriate to my soul growth these doors should remain closed. At the same time I ask that the door of my future should be wide open so that I can walk forward with confidence.

I have always found this to be a most reliable form of focusing. If you follow this suggestion, you then need to be ready and willing to release those things or people which are now no longer part of your path and move on.

It is not wrong to question the intuition in order to clarify the message. It *is* wrong to question it from an analytical standpoint.

Many people ignore their intuition entirely, preferring to follow the "beat of someone else's drum" leading them further and further from their chosen path.

They may openly mistrust their intuition as it appears illogical, failing to follow any obvious socially acceptable patterns of behaviour.

"Let me test it out first and then I'll trust it".
(The first test is to trust it!)

"What if I make a mistake?"
(He who never makes a mistake never lives)

"I can't defend it logically".
(That's the beauty of intuition!)

Failure to listen to the intuition is compounded by the teachings of those in power, such as in areas of religion, politics and parenthood, which stress that there is little space for individual thought if it contradicts that of the group.

Times are changing and as we move into the Aquarian Age it is very important that each individual becomes conscious of their own unique role upon this Earth so that we can work together for a better world. The key to this awareness is the re-connection to our intuition, through our heart and third eye and hence to our inner truth.

Although I agree that it is important to have rules by which order is maintained within the community, these rules must not limit initiative or individual integrity and should be agreed by common consent.

The Piscean Age consisted of the formation of groups maintained by separation.
The Aquarian Age consists of individualisation searching for connection.

At other times the intuitive belief may be contrary to that held by people around you, many of whom are friends. It is easy then to doubt yourself for surely your beliefs must be wrong as the majority is always right.

However, remember the story by *Hans Christian Andersen* concerning the Emperor's New Clothes:

Everybody wanted to please the Emperor by admiring his new garments. Only the little boy, who did not understand the need to please others in order to be loved, saw the truth for, indeed, the Emperor was naked!

Many of the world's greatest achievements have occurred through one man or woman following their intuition against the general tide of opinion.

Intuition is available to every individual on this planet, although many have switched off their intuitive receiver after sharing their insights with others and meeting rejection, isolation, humiliation or the belief that they were mad.

"Don't show yourself up".

"Why would you want to do that?"

"You can't love me if you plan to do this".

"It must be your hormones!"

Indeed for hundreds of years our asylums and mental institutions have been filled with those whose thoughts and ideas do not conform to the social bias, leaving the definition of madness open to abuse.

Because of the fear of rejection, etc. many people completely ignore their higher wisdom preferring to remain within the confines of the belief systems of the tribe.

But some have the courage to listen and start to hear different messages recognising that these touch a note deep inside which cannot be ignored.

At first, the different messages can cause tremendous confusion and even crisis within one's identity as a metamorphosis occurs releasing old belief systems and making way for the new. But, when there is the courage to listen to the small voice within and support from those who have been through the same process, the confusion slowly clears revealing the most beautiful views and a sense of inner peace.

Analogy

There is small community which has lived for hundreds of years at the base of a high mountain. The houses are always in semi-darkness as a thick rain-cloud permanently hovers over the village making the inhabitants believe that this is in fact the sky.

Children are taught that their world consists of this limited space where the light is dim and the air is cool and, since this knowledge has remained unchallenged for generations, the in-built desire to search for another truth has been lost.

One day, a traveller from above the rain-cloud ventures by chance into the little community. At first he is viewed with fear and suspicion but he is friendly for he has no need to threaten the inhabitants as his life is full and rich.

He tells them stories of a beautiful blue sky which stretches as far as the eye can see and a sun which gives light and warmth to all. When it is time to leave, he suggests that some of the community journey with him in order to see these wonderful sights.

But, because they have forgotten how to dream and hence see no purpose in travelling, he leaves alone.

For months the inhabitants talk of their visitor from another place and eventually agree that obviously he had special powers which enabled him to live above the rain-cloud whilst they, of course, were just mere mortals!

Intuition and inspiration are available to everyone, empowering them and allowing greater levels of self-consciousness. And yet for so long we have been taught that we can only receive one radio station on our receiver.

Today, I am telling you that there are many other "radio signals" being sent out on varying frequencies and that all you require is your *own* "radio set", a listening ear and the courage to move the dial away from familiar signals in order to pick up new and exciting impulses.

Have you got that courage to move the dial and respond to the messages you hear even though they may not resonate with the old established patterns?

Are you ready to be responsible for your own life, making choices and decisions from inner knowing rather than from fear or scientifically based logic?

Or will you turn your back on good, personal intuitive advice so that you can continue to meet the needs of your lower self or personality:

"I would love to follow my intuition but my clients need me".

"I know that it is time to stand up for myself but it is far easier to avoid conflict and not make waves. I just want an easy life despite the pain and frustration I feel. These emotions are old friends, don't ask me to face the unknown".

"Honestly (which usually portrays a lie) I know that my intuition says leave him, but I believe that he has the potential to change (and I love the potential not the man)"!

45

Everybody hears their intuition speak, but many choose to ignore it or turn a deaf ear towards it, seeing this as an inconvenient moment to follow its advice.

I relate the illness **tinnitus** (ringing in the ears) to a situation where people fail to listen to their intuition, preferring to ask many questions until they hear an answer which causes minimal disruption and results in little personal responsibility, thereby limiting the risk of making mistakes.

But when you choose to tune into your intuition you will hear different languages, different opinions and different styles, placing you in a stronger position to decide which options resonate with your inner truth and then you will start to dance to your own unique tune. Of course, once each of us is able to tap into our own higher wisdom then there will be less need for the middle man, such as those found within religious organisations, who for so long have been the mediator between the Creator and ourselves.

I believe that the role of these individuals will then return to its original function which was to support and teach people how to reach this higher point of consciousness within themselves without the need for an intermediary.

It is time for each of us to use our intuition wisely and to encourage others to do the same. This may mean that our goals are different but through honest communication based on love, we will recognise that although we walk our separate paths, we are ultimately all joined to the centre of a circle which has no end.

EXERCISES TO ENHANCE THE INTUITION

Intuitive thought may surface during our dreams, in meditation or, more commonly, whilst we are carrying out an action which does not require intense concentration and when we are fairly relaxed.

However, in order to improve the transmission, the following exercises may be helpful:

1) Linking the Heart Centre to the Crown Centre:
Linking Intuition to Inspiration

Sitting comfortably, in a meditative state, imagine standing inside your heart. There is a window in the heart and through it a glorious light is pouring. You feel inspired to seek the source of the light and, finding a door in the heart, you step out into a corridor along which the light is shining.

You walk up the corridor drawn forward by the light until you realise that you are standing totally in the light. You feel the marvellous, energising rays enter every part of your being, every cell of your body, refreshing, healing, renewing, until you are aware that you and the light are one. Enjoy that feeling.

Now it is time to retrace your steps down the corridor but this time you draw the light down the corridor with you. Breathe it down, not allowing it to slip back to its original position.

You step back inside the heart, filling it with this beautiful powerful energy.

The link is now made between heart and crown chakras, between the heart and the head, between the eternal flame and the eternal breath.

Repeat the exercise every day until you can easily imagine a pathway of light between the heart and the top of head. This will ensure enhanced intuitive consciousness.

2) Ask for Help to Listen to and Trust your Intuition

Every morning in meditation, or whatever moment in the day you acknowledge as your time of stillness, ask that you should become more receptive to your intuition and that you should be impressed to follow the information or message you receive.

It often helps to go to the same place in the house and adopt the same bodily posture in order to receive the intuitive information. This is similar to pre-setting the radio to receive specific messages from the intuition and tunes the nervous system to receive the information.

3) Meditating on your Soul Purpose

During your quiet time ask for your soul's purpose over the next month.

Don't let it be too complicated or unachievable and let it involve some fun.

Every day on waking, tell yourself that you are open to any suggestions which will guide you towards your purpose. It may come in the form of a letter, a thought, words spoken by another, something involving the media, in your dream state or during meditation.

Whatever the method or result, check with your heart whether it feels right.

Does it resonate with your inner truth?

Trusting the intuition grows with experience. You may not get it right first time, but you will soon come to have faith in your feelings and inner guidance.

4) Following through on the Message

Have the courage to follow through on the message, however strange or outside your normal mode of action.

It is often best not to share these initial seedling thoughts with everyone for, unless they are on the same wavelength and also work intuitively, it is very easy to be dissuaded from following your own truth.

Keep a note of ideas which have come to you during the day and the action you took in response to the impulse. Also record any result of your action.

Don't be put off if things seem to run into a dead end. You never know where your seeds land when you start to follow your intuition. Seeds sown last year often appear in the most amazing places at a later date.

At the end of the month, look back at the way in which your life's path has moved towards your soul's purpose. You may need to alter this plan slightly for the next month but if you act from the intuition, then you will always attract towards you that which resonates with the heart of your soul and the heart of the Universe.

5) Counting to Ten … Listening to the Inner Voice

For the next seven days allow yourself to count to ten before making any decisions. Ask yourself, is this what my heart desires or am I just going along with other people for the sake of peace and friendship?

Be honest with yourself and others. They may feel that you are rejecting them or their ideas but, if there is true unconditional love between two souls, it is not a matter of either/or but all views and opinions being equally valid.

6) Seeing the Beauty in Others

Choose to be honest with yourself by listening to your intuition and recognising those people who resonate with you and those who do not. You can love everybody but you don't always have to like them!

Rather than criticising others in order to present your opinion, find something good about the person, situation or object and honour this. Remember that although we may not condone someone's actions it does not mean that we reject **them**.

Separate the action from the actor.

There are many paths to the centre of a circle and it is not necessary that we should walk them all or even understand them.

It is more important that we find peace and fulfilment on our path and make space for the actions and opinions of others.

7) **The need to justify suggests that we doubt our beliefs**
Don't fall into the trap of trying to justify your intuitive feelings for this will lead you into a deeper pit of uncertainty. Say as little as possible leaving minimum room for doubt.

8) **Linking the Right and Left brain activity**
If you receive an intuitive thought, speaking it aloud allows the logical language of the left brain to focus the creative ideas of the right brain.

Hopefully there is someone in your life with whom you can share your thoughts. If not, write them down in a journal or record them onto a tape so that you can understand the sequence of thoughts which flow from the intuitive impulse.

We all have the answers to our own problems if only we give ourselves time and space to listen and learn to trust this inner guidance.

Chapter 5

Logic
The Age of Reason

This function of the mind is very familiar to those living in highly developed, technological countries where there is an emphasis on left brain activity and doing rather than being.

It is indeed the strongest function at this time of man's development, emanating from the mental body and applying reason and analysis to our world through scientific examination and research. Therefore, unlike intuition, it is acquired knowledge rather than a sense of inner knowing.

In anatomical terms, the ability to calculate, determine and focus, takes place in the **neocortex** of the brain which is the outer surface of the **cerebral hemispheres**. As its name suggests, it is the newest part of the brain and found only in animals which exhibit high levels of intelligence.

As we will see, the emotions and instincts are associated with other areas of the brain. However, it is not entirely clear which sections to allocate to the intuition or inspiration given that, although the neocortex organises, stores and transmits information, it is not necessarily the source of the impulse.

Diagram 18

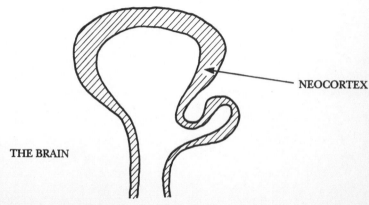

NEOCORTEX

THE BRAIN

The purpose of logic is to organise the intuitive ideas by providing them with shape and structure thus creating a **thought-form**; logic also affords a focus to the uncoordinated energy of emotions by creating a **belief system** so that we might learn from our experiences.

Diagram 19

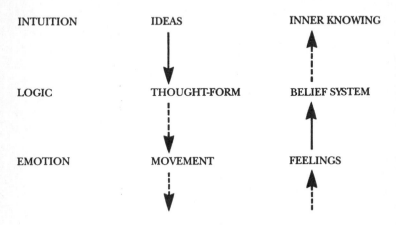

Without the discipline and order provided by logic our intuitive thoughts would never become manifest and our emotions would run riot. Indeed there are many people who allow anxieties, depression, anger and other emotions to rule them rather than stepping back and viewing the situation objectively.

However, too often logic does more than just focus; it also contains, stopping the flow of either intuition or emotions and allows the belief system or thought-form to become the directing force.

Example:

> *When a boyfriend leaves me I feel hurt and rejected. I carry this wound subconsciously into the next relationship which predictably has a similar ending.*
>
> *Now I hold the belief "men reject me" and I may even link this to a deeper belief about myself such as "men reject me because of my weight". Every attempt at dieting is then associated with the fear of being hurt again and the original pain becomes buried beneath a mound of thought-forms which are often far from the truth.*

When we allow the logic to dominate us each experience is then based on proving that which is already known with little space available for spontaneity or growth. There is no room for experimenting or for shades of black and white. Everything either fits into the belief or it does not and if it does not, then it does not exist!

Indeed, the logic can take an idea which is pure fantasy and construct a framework which totally supports its existence.

Experiment:

A group of intelligent and mentally stable psychology students were told that they were to be taken to a mental hospital so that they could observe procedure. At the same time, a team of psychiatric doctors were told that a group of schizophrenic patients were coming to be assessed in terms of prognosis and treatment. The two groups met and, by the end of the day, the doctors were unanimous in their opinion that these patients (psychology students) were so badly affected by the illness that they should receive long-term psychiatric care!

What we believe, we see!

When we have fixed beliefs, hours can be spent in deep discussion arguing a point or criticising the opinions of others without any intention of changing a personal view or considering that there may be another way. It is so easy to criticise but greater intelligence is required not only to come up with an alternative but also to have the courage of one's convictions to turn new thoughts into action.

Talk is cheap . . . . . action costs.

Ideas which are not receiving fresh input either from inspiration or action become stagnant. The emotions, which are the way forward from this impasse, are surrounded by controlling thoughts, often built by those who are frightened of unleashing such irrational, uncontrollable energies.

Diagram 20

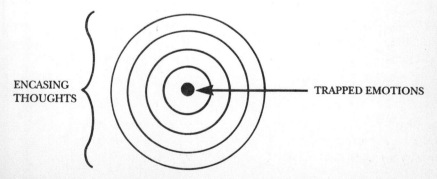

ENCASING
THOUGHTS

TRAPPED EMOTIONS

Eventually the trapped emotion may reveal itself in the form of illness in an attempt to become free with the result that stagnation of creative energy will be reflected in **heart disease** whilst limitation of soul movement will be expressed through **arthritis. Tumours (e.g. cancers, fibroids, breast cysts or boils) and stones (e.g. gall stones and kidney stones)** symbolise the emotion being held tightly within a thought-form. If the emotions are heard and bring about the appropriate change in attitude then the physical manifestation can subside.

However, in many cases, the purpose of the symptom is not recognised and is quickly suppressed with allopathic drugs or orthodox thinking, leading to further energy entrapment. Eventually, the build up of pressure will make its presence known until complete release is achieved, one way or another!

Another common means of releasing trapped emotional energy is through a **panic attack** where the body chooses to be no longer controlled by reasonable, logical thought and gives vent to releasing its energy through every means available!

Diagram 21

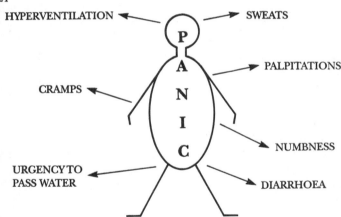

The last 15 years has seen an increase in the desire to place all uncomfortable feelings in "boxes", spurred on by the philosophy of the New Age movement which encourages its followers to move beyond feelings into acceptance.

Example:

"How did you feel when your husband left you for a younger woman?"
"I coped" (which means that, as long as I was paddling madly, I kept my head above water and made myself and others believe that I was calm and still).
"Yes, but how do you feel now?"

"Well, I think he needed to find himself".
"But he left you with no money? How do you feel?"
"It is a learning experience for all of us".
"How do you feel?".
"Well he had a difficult childhood".
"How do you fee-e-el?"

Six weeks later the wife develops asthma and catarrh both of which are strongly linked to unexpressed feelings.

Sometimes we need to deal with trauma by placing it in a box short-term until we are ready to face the underlying emotion, but when things are left in a box for too long, they can start to fester. Perhaps now is a good time to start to clear out some of your cupboards and boxes possibly with professional psychological guidance and determine to start life afresh, unburdened by the past.

For some people life is purely "matter"; created through the application of logic. What you see, touch and own is reality and everything must be done to maintain this illusion.

In other words, in a non-creative cycle, the result only aims to intensify the thought-form or belief system.

"This is what I believe in and therefore I will protect it with my life".

Such beliefs encompass:

1) Religious allegiance.
2) Political allegiance.
3) Social, moral and cultural training, eg. children should look after their aged parents.
4) Belief about oneself, eg. I am clever/stupid/pretty/ugly/I'll never succeed/I'll always get what I want/I am always right.
5) Position in society, eg. only by working hard can I be a useful member of the community.
6) Those based on the role of men and women, eg. men should go out to work to earn money in order to support the family.
7) Those based on security, eg. as long as I have money in the bank, nothing can go wrong. Or, as long as I am in debt nobody can expect too much from me!
8) Global observations, eg. God will provide (but not always the way you want!).
9) New Age thinking.

10) Psychological assessments based on one person's perception of another.

We all need belief systems to act as the foundation on which to build our future, but such beliefs need to allow for growth, for change when necessary and for exploration into new avenues of thought.

If we become obsessed by the form which we have created, we fail to realise that however solid our material world may seem it is but a collection of energy around a particular focus and can be transformed within a moment by a single breath.

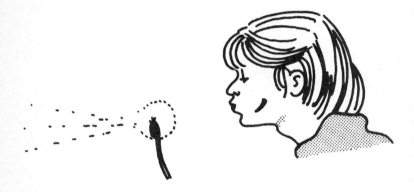

When the hurricane passed through England in 1987, it was the solid oak and beech trees which fell to the ground whilst the more flexible larches and willows bent to the winds of change. How symbolic for a country built on the foundation of being a great Empire that the "big trees are falling" as we move towards a world of co-operation and communication.

While logic controls the show, allowing neither intuition nor emotions to act, we find people who are scared to step into the mirror of life.

It is easy to recognise these individuals in meetings. Their arms are either folded across their solar plexus for protection or sometimes one hand cradles the chin with a finger across the mouth. The body language described latterly denotes *"I'll listen to what you have to say, but I don't believe a word!"*.

They often look bored and they may in fact fall asleep during the meeting. Their non-verbal communication says "I know all this. Tell me something new".

Another trick they employ is to ask a question which is tangential to the line of discussion allowing the individual to expound on a subject of their choosing which has nothing to do with the original text.

I often wonder why such people attend meetings and see someone who would like to appear confident and all-together, but who actually comes across as rigid, frightened to move and often hiding a deep fear of being out of control. Sadly their sense of power is usually limited to acquired knowledge and they rarely understand that the greater intelligence waits within and is called wisdom.

Unfortunately, this attitude can also be found within spiritual circles where spiritual pride or arrogance is seen in those who take every opportunity to express their esoteric knowledge often with a degree of superiority or aloofness whilst failing to put into practice what they preach.

"Those who know don't talk
Those who talk don't know"

(Tao Te Ching, Lao-tzu)

If you think you know it all,
you haven't even started your education.

These and other similar individuals usually prefer to stay within the confined space they know, securing this position by building around them a dogma which demands the allegiance of others, which is often achieved through threats and intimidation.

Analogy

There is a group of people who have lived in a room for a long time. Through the windows they see others walking in the sunshine, playing with children, and adapting to the changing seasons with enthusiasm and a sense of adventure. From the inside these changes are threatening and they reassure themselves that they should stay in the room by commenting:

"Look at those people enjoying themselves, they should know better".

"They must be careful of the sun's rays, we have been told they are damaging".

"Did you see how those people were playing with the children? No responsibility, no values. If they are not careful, the children will believe that life is fun".

Even though each of them may have a secret desire to move out of the room and into the sunshine, each is afraid of stepping into the unknown and therefore uses the group as a reason to stay.

"If I left, the group or individuals within it could not survive or cope without me".

"I would not want to hurt the others and appear to be suggesting that what they are doing is wrong. Therefore I'll stay".

"I don't want to be alone and therefore I will stay in the room even though there is a part of me which longs to leave".

"My thoughts are different from my friends' but I need to belong to a group therefore I will conform".

"I must be wrong because these people are always right!"

In the end, nobody ever leaves the room; nobody ever experiences the exquisite aroma of Nature nor the wind on their face. Not one of them understands the creative energy of play or that spiritual growth occurs through emotional expression.

Their bodies reflect their rigidity of mind. Between them they experience arthritis, heart disease, kidney stones, diabetes and panic attacks. Each illness attempts to present a picture by which they can understand what is happening within their mind but, because of the fear of change, the disease represents a crisis rather than an opportunity for transformation.

This story is repeated time and time again in industry, welfare, education and government. Systems are assembled, based on inspirational ideas, but once the structure is in place, there needs to be room for new development and initiative. However, this can only occur if the organisation is able to be objective to that which it has just created.

If our life is dependent on that creation, linked to the belief that life is purely form and not inspiration, then we will do all in our power to maintain a system which is out-of-date and unproductive.

Anybody with new thinking will then threaten the status quo created by the tribal energy and be made to feel that they are wrong, out of line or persuaded to keep quiet by threats to their job or reputation.

Until we realise that creation is based on evolution and involution, on build up and break down, we will be forever plastering over old cracks and living in a make-believe world that all is well.

Those who live by an unswerving belief system often become boring bureaucrats who are uninspiring and arrogant.

This same situation is found in many of the new groups which are emerging at this time with the overall power being given to a guru or teacher whose authority is maintained through mysticism, fear, charm or the promise of financial reward.

This is the *old way*. The Piscean Age of the last 2000 years was based on the understanding that there should be a leader who must be followed in a way similar to shoals of fish swimming in accordance with those in the lead.

Diagram 22

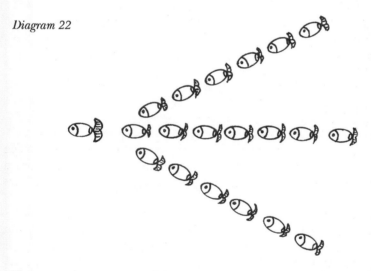

However, the message of the Aquarian Age is that each should follow his or her own path with the understanding that, with individual uniqueness, everybody has something to offer and that we will soon come together in common unity (or community) to share our gifts in order to bring about Universal wholeness.

Diagram 23

The age of the guru is over as is the denial of responsibility for one's actions and thoughts. Now is the time for observation of one's inner impulses so that these may be brought into manifestation through love for the good of all mankind.

It is also time to acknowledge and accept that it is through our thoughts and belief systems that our outer world is shaped and that we create our own reality. We cannot grow spiritually when we are so fearful of letting go of old out-dated beliefs, refusing to recognise anything which does not fit into our logical, scientific opinions.

So I ask you to look at your belief systems and see where you are limited and where you would be happy to make some changes. It is interesting to speculate how we, as multi-dimensional free thinkers, ever allowed ourselves to become so restricted by Earthly patterns of thought and behaviour.

It would be easy to blame those in authority for this situation but we must ask ourselves why were we so eager to give away our power in the first place?

We have reached a stage when we need to reassess our belief systems realising that feelings such as pain, hurt, disappointment and resentment are purely the result of separation from our own inner truth. It is time to re-evaluate what we truly want from life and, more importantly, what we are prepared to give.

Either change the belief or change your attitude
. . . . we are the masters of our own destiny.

I do not believe that this is a planet of suffering, pain, guilt or persecution. These are man-made rules which need to be discarded. But before we build another set of conditions let each of us reach inside and touch the heart of our being so that we may be open to our intuitive thoughts and build a healthier, happier and more unified world for all concerned.

When our thoughts are not employed fruitfully they will of their own accord look for other ways to act. This means that if our attention is not fixed onto any particular focus we will often create a problem to satisfy our restless mind.

"What can I worry about now?"

Would it not be better to give the mind the opportunity to work on something far more creative and pleasurable.

"What can I be excited about?"

Don't waste your thoughts on issues which are not important to your soul growth.

Sometimes we even use the creative energy of our logic to produce a very realistic outcome to a hypothetical fantasy.

Example:

Your husband is five minutes late home from work.
"That's it; he has had an accident.
I told him he should check the car before he went out this morning. He is so laid-back and never listens to me.
Which hospital have they taken him to?
Oh, I hope they haven't taken him there!
I'll have to go and see him. What shall I do with the children? My parents will have to come over.
What if he has died? What will we do?
The children will have to leave that school.
. . . . . Maybe I will meet someone new!
That's a nice thought!"

Two minutes later your husband arrives home, after having been held up in a traffic jam.

In less than a minute we have often lived a whole lifetime which seems real and yet is pure fantasy.

If you don't believe this to be true, watch your thoughts for half-an-hour and see how far they travel.

We can find ourselves worrying needlessly over something which may never happen, spurred on by the fact that one day it could. Here we experience "rational irrational" thoughts which defy any attempts at dissolution.

Unfortunately, since thought creates reality, that which you dwell upon in your mind may well become manifest. One of the ways to prevent this is to use the wonderful phrase suggested by *Susan Jeffers* in her book "*Feel the Fear and do it anyway*" and say "I'll deal with it when it happens".

Our mind is very creative and enjoys the chance to wander into areas which as yet are just a dream. But there are times and places to dream and it is important that we should set aside minutes or hours in the day for silent reflection and meditation, otherwise we find that our mind wanders at inappropriate times.

Remember when you were driving and could not recall passing along a section of road? Where was your mind then?

How often does your mind wander when listening to someone else speak, triggered by something they have said? Where does your mind go?

We owe it to fellow travellers and those who speak to us that we are fully present in that moment and recognise the importance of silence for inner work.

From an esoteric point of view logic is focused mainly through the throat chakra which is related to self-expression and self-creativity. It provides a passage for the thought-forms and beliefs which originate from the higher mind and the emotions respectively.

However, if logic limits the flow from either of these sources then predictably I see problems in the area of the throat, ears, breathing or thyroid gland. The message of these diseases is that the spontaneous creative expression of the soul is being repressed by the analytical mind.

The blocked energy may indeed start to affect the third eye, which is the chakra above the throat, and produce visual problems and headaches. During my Workshops, where I offer innovative ways of thinking and acting, it is not uncommon for one or two participants to develop headaches.

In my experience this usually represents a degree of resistance to ideas which are touching into an inner truth and yet if implemented will require change.

In order to reduce the level of disharmony in these areas there is a need to "let go" and allow "Thy will" to dominate over "my will" thereby using logic in a more appropriate manner.

Emotions relate to the element of water, logic relates to fire. As the thinking process becomes the main function of the mind we are seeing more and more people analysing every situation, planning every move until the "fire" becomes so hot that they literally "burn out" with exhaustion.

The fire (logic) needs to be combined with water (emotions) and contained by earth (instincts) so that it does not burn out of control. If you always start your conversation with "I think", could it be time to bring more water and earth into your life?

As the fire of our mental body becomes more active and acts upon the water of our emotions, we will see the production of increasing quantities of "mist and steam". The effect of this is to reduce the visibility of well-known landmarks which have guided us for so long, leaving us feeling confused and disorientated.

Many will experience anxiety and frustration when this occurs and yet within the mist there is an opportunity for tremendous growth and transformation. We are presently in the *fifth root race* of mankind which is known as the *Aryan* race where the logical mind is highly developed and is ready to be used to focus the incoming soul impulses in conjunction with the other levels of consciousness.

One of the major challenges in the years ahead, if we are to prevent increased mental illness, dementia and exhaustion in our society, is to allow logic to expand our thinking and not contract it. The rapid increase in computer and communication technology which has taken place around the world over the last decade is symbolic of the tremendous growth which is taking place within our own mental capacity. We are now able to make faster connections, retain more knowledge and process more complex concepts than our ancestors.

This skill should be used wisely; it is important that knowledge and information are not held as a possession or as a weapon of power but rather applied wherever it can be of service to ourselves or others, always combined with the richness of wisdom and compassion.

EXERCISES TO FOCUS THE LOGIC

1) **Exploring the Belief Systems**
   Ask yourself the questions:

a) Whose beliefs do you follow?
b) Are they formulated from your own experience or are they purely hand-downs from other people?
c) Are they still appropriate today?
d) Are they workable?
e) Do they bring you happiness and fulfilment?
f) How easy is it for others to connect with you in harmony?
g) Who decides what is right in your life?
h) Do you fight to defend your ideals?
i) If so, how secure are you in their merits?
j) When did you last test out a belief to see if it still applies? (Or is that too frightening to contemplate).
k) Is it important to you that you are always right or are there other ways which may be equally appropriate in different circumstances?
l) Do you always have to have the last word?

Having listened to your answers you may choose to review your belief systems and ask yourself what is important **now** and what can be released into the past.

You may in fact wish to incorporate new standards and values into your set of beliefs recognising that on-going minor adjustments are essential so that you may continue to grow and transform.

2) Listening to our Language

Many of our deep seated beliefs originate far beyond our lifetime and were passed down through the generations.

Through our language and through our actions we protect them from dissolution or investigation:

"It's too difficult"
"I can't change"
"I must do it this way"
"But how could I manage?"
"It is easy for you to say/do that"
"This is the way it is".
"Life is so difficult!"
"I'm not like that".

When we speak these words, our mind and body hears . . . no change! No need to threaten a comfortable/uncomfortable status quo.

What is **your** language?

Listen to yourself, especially under stress. What excuses do you make to stay exactly where you are however intolerable the situation?

If I want to change my beliefs and hence my actions and behaviour, I have to change my language.

"It's too difficult" becomes *"what an exciting challenge"*.

"I can't change" becomes *"I'm ready for transformation"*.

Whatever your language, it should support you and lead you towards expansion of your being. If it doesn't, change your vocabulary.

And I am not necessarily talking about affirmations. You can stand in front of a mirror and say a thousand times;

"I am beautiful, I am beautiful, I am beautiful, I am beautiful . . . . .".

And a little voice says: *"No, you're not!"* and these four little words annihilate any previous positive thoughts.

Change the way you look at life rather than trying to cover up what is uncomfortable to accept.

3) Body work for the Over-analytical Mind

You cannot treat the logical mind *with* the logical mind. If someone is extremely logical and always analyses everything before speaking or acting, then psychotherapy is not always the most appropriate treatment.

To allow the mind to move, you often have to work on the body first. Therefore I usually recommend patients to attend a massage therapist or body worker who will work on the physical form where memories are held and start to loosen trapped energy which can be used for a more creative process.

4) Letting go through Movement or Song

Another wonderful way of letting go of uninspiring thoughts is through song, dance, movement or other forms of art. Try holding onto an anxiety or worry whilst belly-dancing or singing from the top of your lungs. It is not easy!

And, afterwards, it's hard to remember what it was that you were worrying about.

5) Using the Logical Mind creatively

When you have an idea, whether from the intuition or inspiration, write it down; already your logical mind has been brought into activity.

Then allow yourself time to lay down some details and plans related to the idea:

"What do I need to do in order to bring this idea to fruition?"

"Who do I know who can help me to move forward with this idea?"

"Where can I go to gain more knowledge about the subject?"

"When would be the best time to promote my idea?"

"How do I maintain excellence in the management of this idea?"

At last the logical mind is really happy. All these beautiful questions to be answered, details to be given and a focus for one's present purpose in life. What joy!

Chapter 6

Emotions
Breakdown to Breakthrough

This is a function of the mind which requires little description for most of us are very aware of the range of emotions available even though some of them may be outside our own repertoire.

The primary emotions are joy, fear, sadness and anger and can act as both the force to motivate and the feeling in response to an action.

Example:
"I speak to this person in anger".
Or "I feel really angry about this situation".
"I happily do my work".
Or "I feel very happy at what has taken place."

The motivating emotional force embraces the rather austere thought form and expands it with the use of design and movement, thereby intensifying the creative effect of the original idea.

It is as if the emotions surround the thought and through their movement and flexibility expand and transform it into something of substance.

Diagram 24

THOUGHT → THOUGHT → SUBSTANCE

ENCOMPASSING EMOTION   THOUGHT IN ACTION

Think of a time when you added passionate emotion to your desire to achieve something and remember the end result. Imagine if you had said the same words but without the energy. It is probable that the result would have been very different.

Emotions are a powerful force of creation and, when used with the right intention, can enhance the outcome of our dreams.

The emotional decoration used to intensify the reaction may include the clothes we choose to wear, our style of movement, the use of facial expression, the tone of our voice, the posture we adopt or our hand movements which may reach out and touch someone we love.

It is as if there is an emotional dressing-up store which allows us to take any "clothes" we require for a particular scene, returning them afterwards and choosing new "clothes" for the next performance.

This wonderful assortment of emotions provides the world and its inhabitants with a myriad of creative possibilities for every situation.

Without emotions we are flat, ill-defined and robotic.

Diagram 25

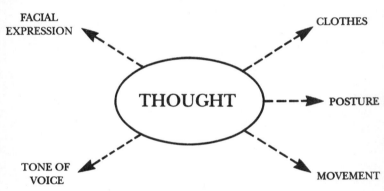

The emotional energy is linked through consciousness to our inner free spirit which exists beyond the limitations of our three-dimensional world and is willing to give spontaneously expecting nothing in return. This same free spirit is present in intuition where the motivating force is the higher power of love.

Such spontaneity and commitment to the present moment without expectations of the future can be seen in the emotions of young children.

Example:

Remember the last time you watched children play.

One moment they were squabbling over the ownership of a favourite toy, accompanied by tears of frustration, and the next the toy is abandoned, the tears disappear and there is a wild whoop of excitement as something new catches their attention.

Whether fighting over the toy or seeing something new the emotions were real in both situations. However, as soon as one event ended, the accompanying emotion disappeared to be replaced by another.

Emotions provide design and movement
. . . . . but in themselves have no substance.

The other side of the coin is the feeling part of our emotions which emerges in response to our participation in some activity or relationship.

Diagram 26

BELIEF

FEELINGS

ACTION / RELATIONSHIP

Feelings are an internal awareness almost impossible to define except in terms of bodily sensations or by the use of logic when we match the sensation to a memory.

Example:

I feel uncomfortable talking to this person
I experience an inner trembling
My breathing is becoming short and shallow
My forehead starts to sweat
The muscles on the back of my neck are tightening
My mouth is tightly closed and the muscles in my jaw are cramping
My hands are clenched
I feel as if I am about to explode

Memory:

Last time I felt this way I was angry, therefore:
I believe that I am once again angry.
Now I have the chance to respond.

Some people don't need the analysis and just explode whilst others nurse all these sensations for days eventually concluding:

"I think I was angry 10 days ago!"

Feelings are the synthesis of all sensory input gleaned from our outer senses, from our sixth sense (psychic sensitivity) and from the hormones circulating around the body. This package is then linked with memory from previous lives, with cell memory and with soul memory to provide the energy of a feeling.

Anatomically, emotional information is stored in an area of the brain called the limbic system which networks with major sensory centres such as the hypothalamus (which directs all hormones) and the thalamus (which receives information from the outside world). The limbic system lies between the neocortex of the logic and the reptilian brain of the instincts, both of which hold memories from the past.

Diagram 27

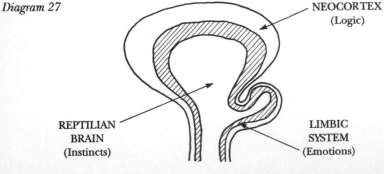

NEOCORTEX
(Logic)

REPTILIAN
BRAIN
(Instincts)

LIMBIC
SYSTEM
(Emotions)

The purpose of feeling is to attract our attention towards a particular event which, on a subconscious level, has been decreed invaluable for soul growth.

Just as the emotions are the container for the transformation of thought into creative activity, so the feelings encompass an event into our consciousness in order that we may grow and transform on the level of the personality and the soul.

Diagram 28

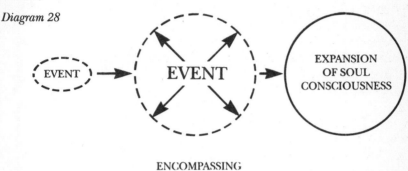

ENCOMPASSING
FEELINGS

Example:

I spend a really pleasant evening with some friends.
I feel happy and embody the energy of the evening into my being.
In this way I increase my understanding in respect of feeling joy in my life and my soul consciousness expands.

Our outwardly moving emotions and inwardly focused feelings open us up to new experiences so that we may incorporate new energy into our life, whether this is coming from our higher mind or from the world outside.

Diagram 29

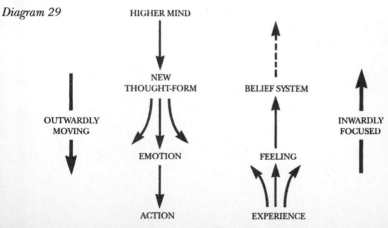

Analogy

The emotions are like a doorway between one room and another. When you are in room A you have a certain identity and set of belief systems. You then step into the doorway where the bonds holding the old structure loosen, creating a relatively nebulous form within which change can occur.

When you are ready, you step from the doorway into room B where you take on an entirely new form, built from the seeds of the previous identity.

Diagram 30

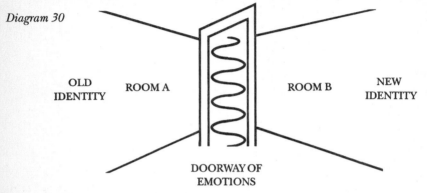

DOORWAY OF
EMOTIONS

Emotions are a process of transformation essential to life but are in themselves without form.
A doorway does not exist except as a meeting place between two rooms.

As the bonds of the old form loosen, a vulnerability occurs which can create anxiety. However, without this relaxation of structure, no growth can occur.

Example:

When a lobster or crab wishes to grow in size, it first has to shed its outer shell leaving it temporarily vulnerable and unprotected.

And yet only during this sensitive stage can the inner form take on more food and expand in size to its new potential.

When the appropriate growth is achieved, a hard shell develops around the expanded form and the crustacean moves away.

Feelings and emotions are the unstructured container of change. When used appropriately, and with the purpose of soul growth, we can experience tremendous shifts in consciousness especially when joy and love are the motivating force.

Analogy

A chrysalis is the stage of transformation between the earth-bound caterpillar and the beautiful free-flying butterfly.

In itself, the chrysalis, wrapped in its cocoon, is relatively unstructured and yet it is in this state that metamorphosis and magic occur.

One of the commonest episodes of transformation in our life is that of grief when it is necessary for us to move from one scenario to another. During this time the bonds holding the old situation loosen through the use of a variety of emotions which may include anger, blame, guilt, joy and confusion.

The purpose of these emotions is to shift energy so that eventually a state of acceptance is reached. At the same time there are dramatic changes in the consciousness of the individual who, like it or not, will be forced to review the direction of their life and make the appropriate changes.

Breakdown to Breakthrough.

Unfortunately, it is not uncommon to become stuck in one phase of the emotional breakdown so that we continue to act from a nebulous position rather than being enriched or strengthened by the event.

Whenever our emotions are involved, change will occur.
But the emotions are transitional not permanent.

Without a clear directive in the doorway of the emotions it is easy to become lost, fearful of going forward and unable to go back. Unfortunately, the longer we stay in this place of uncertainty and turmoil, the more familiar it becomes and soon we believe that this is reality.

In this amorphous state we may even relinquish our individual integrity, unable to maintain boundaries especially in relationships, often becoming "pleasers" or victims of life.

We are now lost in the mirror of life:

"Things always happen to make me feel sad."

"People make me angry all the time."

"I only feel good when other people are happy".

We become reactors to life's experiences rather than actors.

Life is then built around this great illusion which says:

"As soon as I feel anything, I will react rather than ever allowing the more stable and objective views of the logic and intuition to interject."

In this way we block any new thought or inspiration and achieve a cycle of living based purely on emotions and feelings, attracting towards us situations which by design can only perpetuate the cycle.

Example:

I am inspired to produce something and use my emotions to achieve this. I'm delighted with the result and enjoy the feeling of happiness.

This leads me to produce something else so that I can feel happy again and in time receive the same satisfaction.

Eventually, I so enjoy the feeling that I do anything to produce the identical result, happiness. I no longer care if the product is useful or whether indeed it may harm others.

All I care is that I feel happy.

Diagram 31

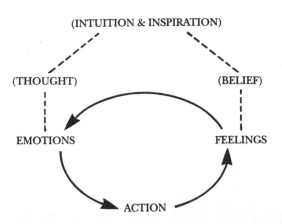

In this scenario we become obsessed with the feeling rather than the purpose or the result. The intention is to feel happy and that is all that matters.

Our identity and purpose in life are now bound to this feeling and it is no longer just *desirable* to feel this way but a *necessity*. We become this feeling and without it believe we will not survive.

So, in the same way as some people are addicted to external drugs in order to feel a certain way, others are addicted to their emotions for similar reasons.

The crazy thing is that many individuals don't even have the pleasure of feeling happy, for their addiction is to other emotions such as fear, anger, resentment, bitterness or sadness.

Such emotions are fortified by the logical mind which produces a belief system to maintain the illusion.

Example:
I feel terrified when I have to give a presentation at work. My hands sweat and my heart pounds but surprisingly the talk is a great success.
My logic initially says "Even when I'm terrified, I can do well" but after similar episodes it changes to "When I am terrified I do well".
Now I need the anxiety in order to perform, and although my physical body starts to complain, I cannot back down for I know of no other way of acting.

The emotion becomes the driving force, reinforced by a belief system which is constantly being proved by the experiences I attract towards myself.

i.e. *"When I am terrified I do well".*

Much of this process occurs on a subconscious level for most people would be ashamed to admit to the role their emotions play in the organization of their life, even though it is obvious to everybody else.

This emotional force, often used extremely subtly, leads to "power games" between individuals, described so beautifully in "*The Celestine Prophecy*". These games can be played *ad infinitum* as long as neither player acknowledges their dependency on their emotions for identity and survival.

During the "contest" it is important to gain control by creating a state of powerlessness in the other person through the use of complex emotions such as guilt, fear, withdrawal, criticism, victim or pity:
"I thought you loved me?"
"You must do as I say or I will . . . ."
"I don't want to talk about it."

"Why don't you act like other people?"
"Don't pick on me. It's nothing to do with me."
"I feel so sorry for you."

Many people deny their participation in these games thereby creating an even wider chasm between their own inner truth and the great illusion:

"I'm not jealous, but why does she always need to tell me about her good fortune."
"I'm not criticising, I only want the best for them."
"It's not that I'm a victim, it's just that people always seem to put obstacles in my way".

Unless we are willing to look into the mirror with honesty and see our own reflection, we will continue to delude ourselves that the problems are outside and that we have no responsibility for our own life.

There is more to life than games. Wake up to the truth.

What was meant to provide us with colour, movement and change ends up trapping us in our own desires. The soul's purpose is forgotten and logic and rationale are avoided for they may persuade us away from a "drug" to which we are addicted.

Our addiction unfortunately is intensified each time we tell our "story". In order to break the cycle, we need to seek the help of someone who can provide us with the skills to use our emotions to *change* the situation/belief, rather than to fortify it.

Analogy

The emotions are like a shadow which appears when we are not standing precisely under the sun. The message of the shadow is that we should move so that we may receive the sun's rays directly.

When we move the shadow disappears.

Too many people spend all their time examining the shadow never realizing that it is not the shadow which is important but its message. When we look beyond our limited perspective of life we can see the total picture.

The shadow is an illusion directing us towards reality.
... the emotions have no substance but are essential for soul growth.

There is a time for being in the doorway or the shadow and a time for moving on. There is a time to be in a cocoon and a time to become a butterfly.

The present social situation encourages emotional dependency, many people believing that to suffer is noble or that life is a struggle. Indeed it is easy to feel an "inadequate failure" if you have no story to tell!

We are at an important period in our evolution when we need to recognize the value of our emotions without becoming addicted to the suffering.

You are not your emotions
... they are but a passing moment.

And there seem to be socially acceptable emotions and those which are frowned upon. Being happy and enjoying life is definitely discouraged!

"It won't last"
"Don't be too happy. I just don't want to see you hurt."
"Are you alright? You are smiling again."

Life is for enjoying so smile!

I strongly believe that releasing our dependency on an emotion is far more difficult than releasing our dependency on chemicals such as nicotine and alcohol for most of us have an ingrained belief that if we want something the only power available to us is through the emotions.

What we fail to understand is that the greatest power in our world is love. But this love is not that linked to our personal desires but to that which transcends our needs and is reached through intuition and inspiration.

Love links all the functions of the mind so that they work in harmony, strengthening its influence. It is true to say that there may be fewer outward manifestations associated with love, ie. movement of body and changes in the voice, but the inner feeling is magnificent and almost beyond expression.

True love just is.

I recognize four levels of emotions commonly expressed:

Top layer:	*"I feel very angry at what happened."*
Second layer:	*"I feel very hurt by the event."*
Third layer:	*"I'm terrified he'll leave me."*
Fourth layer:	*"I joyfully surrender my emotions to the power of love".*

In many ways, we cannot reach that state of surrender without passing through the emotional layers. Mastering our emotions is not related to ignoring them or placing them in hidden boxes.

It is only when we can become friends with the emotions and experience their power without becoming dependent upon them that we can eventually reach Nirvana.

The link between emotion and dependency has been reinforced by scientific research which shows that when we experience any emotion many of our cells, including the white blood cells, and the brain release chemicals called neuropeptides into the fluids of the body.

These messengers are similar to hormones which are released from the endocrine glands, the best known being the endorphins which are natural morphines bringing lightness, euphoria and absence of pain to the individual.

As with any chemical, it is easy for the body and mind to become dependent on its presence and this is possibly one of the reasons why it is so hard to release the emotion once created.

Each emotion has its own particular neuropeptide and for a period of time this circulates in the fluids of our body (eg. blood, tears, saliva) spreading the word about our present state of mind.

"Watch out guys, she's got out of bed on the wrong side!"

When we express our emotions appropriately to **the right person** at **the right time** then these neuropeptides eventually leave our body. However, if our emotions become chronic, and this is estimated at five days, then the chemicals start to influence the cells in a negative fashion, leading eventually to physical illness.

Experiment:
Researchers worked with a group of actors who were known to be able to express their emotions with reasonable sincerity.

Initially they were told that their performances in the auditions were brilliant and that they were to be given the leading role in a play. The actors expressed joy and happiness which, when a blood sample was taken, was found to have enhanced the immune response.

Later they were told that their auditions were so poor that they should leave the theatre. They started to cry and were unhappy.

However, the repeated blood test gave a surprising result. Instead of the expected poor response it was found that once again the immune response was enhanced by these sad emotions.

The same result occurred with fear and anger.
(Margaret Kemeny; *Healing and the Mind 1993*)

As long as the emotion is appropriate and expressed at the right time there is a rise in the ability of the body to cope with infections and tumours and an increase in the person's well-being.

However, long-term emotion, especially depression, has been seen to depress the immune system. Such extended emotions include:

Fear . . . to . . . frustration and anxiety
Anger . . . to . . . resentment and bitterness
Sadness . . . to . . . despair and depression
Joy . . . to . . . mania

Think of your own life:
Do you hold onto old hurts and grudges which belong to the past?
Do you spend hours in worry and frustration?
Do you have a sense of loss and failed fulfilment?
Do you constantly feel guilty?

If the answer is "yes" to any of those questions it is time for change and to release old pains realizing that:
1) Old grudges hold us back from new opportunities for growth. It is time to let go and move on.

2) Think what you are missing by staying in the sadness or despair. There are many who love you wishing only to see you happy again.

3) Look at your talents and gifts. Where can they be used for the benefit of yourself and others?

4) Where can you find joy in your life even if it is for just a few minutes a day?

5) If you experience guilt recognise that its only purpose is to alter your actions in the future. The past is over, forgive yourself and start to live again.

An emotion which most people experience at some time in their life but which is rarely discussed is depression, often described as "feeling low" or "being down". It can be seen as a state of numbness where there is no movement and it appears as if the person's "train" has left the main track and is now sitting in a siding.

Depression, which is well-known for reducing the immune reaction, may appear as excessive tiredness, aching muscles, irritability, mood swings, sleep problems and appetite changes. There are also feelings of being unable to cope and lack of motivation.

Whereas I appreciate that there are some cases when expert psychiatric help is required, for the majority of people who have a "down day", I suggest that they "do it in style". Get out the black clothes, the candles, the saddest movies or music, the handkerchiefs, a large box of chocolates and wallow!

Enjoy it!

Motivating yourself to act in this state will put you back on track and then you can decide if you want to stay there or not. Of course, there will always be people who are happy being miserable and their decision needs to be respected if not entirely understood.

The uncontrolled aspect of the emotions can greatly upset those who are more logically minded and can see no place in their life for such spontaneous activity.

Such individuals may well prefer to stay on the edge of the mirror fearful of stepping inside where they may have to lose control or risk change. These people tend to be guided significantly by their logic holding onto their beliefs however dubious their origins.

They may attract sympathy and attention from *rescuers* who are looking for lost souls, but will rebuff any rescue plan and feel deeply offended by the apparent criticism that they are not happy in their present state.

The best form of support is to love and accept others wherever they choose to stay whilst at the same time asking ourselves:

"Who needs to change?"

At the same time, those who choose to stay outside the mirror need to recognise that others may wish to move and extend the same love and understanding to them.

In evolutionary terms, the emotions flourished in the *fourth root race* which was exemplified in the *Atlantean* Civilisation. This culture was highly developed technically and existed upon this Earth from approximately 25,000 BC until its demise in the Great Flood around 8,500 BC.

By awakening the emotions through the activation of the solar plexus chakra, mankind developed free-will as the first step towards self-consciousness and taking responsibility for individual contribution to the planet.

However, once given the power of the emotions to transform thoughts and ideas, many of the Atlanteans lost sight of the Greater Plan and only became concerned with their desires. They used this power and knowledge against others and eventually destroyed themselves by their own greed.

Many of the ideas of that time are re-emerging today especially in the fields of medicine, science, religion and spirituality. Let us hope that higher wisdom guides the application of this ancient knowledge so that individual desires are superseded by those for the Universe.

Emotions are essential for spiritual growth for it is within this state that we can enter the space of childlike innocence, loosen the bonds of old redundant identities and allow the magic of miracles to take place.

Enjoy the experience!

EXERCISES TO ENJOY THE EMOTIONS
1) Acting rather than Reacting
Some people are reactors and some never react at all! A reactor is someone who does not think between feeling and action, immediately connecting the feeling to an old belief system or memory and reacting accordingly.

Some burst into tears whilst others run off, go quiet, sulk or let rip with their anger. Whatever the method, the subconscious desire is to dis-empower other people thereby increasing one's own strength. This is playing the game of power (*The Celestine Prophecy*).

If you don't believe this is true, imagine what it would be like if the other person was not present. Sure, the situation would not have occurred in the first place, but I wonder how much of your reaction is for effect?

Of course some people can react on their own but usually they get the opportunity to let others know just how terrible they felt yesterday! *"But I don't want to burden you with my problems!"*

The only way to break the cycle is first to admit to yourself that you are playing games.

Then decide to change your pattern by doing something different next time.

Example:
a) Take a deep breath and count to ten before speaking.
b) Walk away from the situation or, if you always do this, stay.
c) Have the courage to say: "I'm not going to play this game".
d) Ask the person who appears to want to hurt you, if this is true. (More often than not we don't hear correctly and only hear what we believe to be true.)
e) Tell people how you feel without the need to justify your feelings.
f) If one person always seems to dis-empower you, choose to change the interaction rather than just sit there and inwardly complain, eg. get up and move, change your expression, tell them how you feel, stop seeing them or do something a little crazy which would certainly distract them!
g) Recognise that it's the action taken by the other individual which you don't like rather than the actor themselves. When everything becomes extremely personal we lose sight of the wider perspective and cannot act rationally.

One of the commonest reasons for failing to express our emotions is that we don't wish to hurt others. The subconscious reason is that if we hurt others they may not like us and then we would feel rejected. So it is far easier to avoid conflict and not to "rock the boat".

I suggest that there are ways of communicating which allow us to relay our point of view without compromising the integrity of the other individual or our relationship, but they depend on our own sense of self-worth and the intent behind our statement.

If what we say is aimed at hurting the other person then we can only expect an unfavourable response. However, if we speak to the individual as a fellow soul, respecting their path on this Earth, then the result is often very different.

When we come from love, the other person can only feel hurt if that is their choice.

2) **Releasing old Hurts, Pains, etc**

We all have a reasonable idea of where we hold old pains even though the memory has been well hidden from the outside world for many years.

Unfortunately, although we can run away from one situation, whilst the pain is still present, it will attract towards itself new episodes of a similar nature, encouraging us to heal the original wound.

This is not necessarily an exercise that can be done without psychotherapeutic help, for sometimes we bring to the surface issues which require long-term professional support.

However, there are some situations which are less traumatic and where grudges are still held.

In these cases, I fully recommend writing a letter you never send to the person who has aggrieved you telling them of your feelings. At the end of the letter you may wish to add something related to completing this emotional tie which does not necessarily mean the end of the relationship.

When you are ready, burn the letter allowing it to be taken into the ether to reach the higher consciousness of all concerned.

You can even write a letter to someone who has died or passed over telling them what you were unable to say when they were alive. Perhaps you just want to send them your love.

Some people send the letter once written. If you do this, then you have to realise that the result may not be as you predicted and you need to be ready to deal with the consequences.

Letting go also means learning to forgive which is easy to say but which can be hard to put into practice especially when it comes to forgiving ourselves. We can in fact only forgive others when we have learnt to love ourselves and received our own forgiveness.

Forgiveness is the end stage to a period of transformation often only reached by passing through a range of emotions requiring professional psychological help.

On many occasions we become hurt and disappointed when other people do not live up to our expectations. Then forgiveness can be expressed in the following manner:

"Forgive me for ever expecting you to be more than you are able to be".
People can only live their own lives not our expectations!

3) Change the Emotions you Experience

We can be so unaware of our emotions that we allow them to run our life without question:

a) *"I worry all the time."*

  "Why? That is just the way I am."

Worry never solved any problems, If you need to worry, sit in a corner every morning for 20 minutes and worry intensively. Then don't worry again until the following morning.

  "That's far too difficult. What will I do for the rest of the day?"

Many anxious people fill their minds with problems which may or may not occur. Decide that you are going to "deal with the situation when it happens" (*Susan Jeffers*) and then find something useful into which you can put all this creative energy (such as helping others).

b) If you are fed up with being miserable and wish to change this state then when you open your eyes in the morning:

  Smile. Say good morning to the day and to your body.

  Think of at least one thing which makes you happy about this day.

  Don't switch on the news! Play some cheerful music.

  Dress for the day not just for convenience.

  Decide you will make one other person smile today.

  If you are near Nature, see what she is offering today as a new gift.

  Make a point of deciding to create your own reality from an inner sense of joy and contentment.

  And, at the end of the day, make a note of why this day was so special and go to sleep with thoughts of gratitude and love.

Life is not all happiness and laughter but I can tell you if you smile, the world smiles back.

c) If you are always angry, ask yourself why you constantly need to be angry. If it is a defence then ask yourself whether you wish to continue this state.

Most times, anger hides hurt or fear. The positive use of anger is to move us towards change or away from an emotionally charged situation. Static defensive anger is only destructive to the user.

If you feel angry decide either to acknowledge the underlying hurt and fear and express it or to move, changing the situation so that you can find some inner peace.

d) Remember the circulating neuropeptides and decide to express your emotions to the **appropriate person** at the **appropriate time**.

Of course there may be occasions when this is impossible so I suggest you express your feelings into a journal, to an empty chair, in the car or on the top of a hill. But **let them go** and resolve to transform the situation next time.

e) Remember that emotions are expressed through a variety of ways:
  The colour and style of your clothes
  The way you walk and your posture
  The manner in which you move your hands
  Your facial expression
  The tone of your voice

If you want to change your emotional state, go back to the emotional "dressing-up" store and pick out some new decoration. Imagine that you are about to take a part in a play and enjoy the experience.

By adding rhythm to your voice or more elaborate hand movements to your repertoire you immediately start to change your mood.

Use the transformational energy of emotions to enhance your life for the better.

Chapter 7

Instincts
Born to Survive

W hen the first human soul entered the Earth it took its physical form from the animal kingdom, receiving at the same time one of the most powerful functions of the mind, the instincts.

Survival skills have been passed down from generation to generation within the DNA of every cell of every organ. Nobody teaches you these skills and, although you may come to understand what triggers the response, the actual mechanism is so swift and automatic that there is no time for logical analysis or even intuitive perception.

Example:

Remember when you were last involved in a near car accident. Within an instant your muscles, nerves and joints, working in perfect unison, applied exactly the right amount of pressure to the pedals, turned the steering wheel with dexterity, provided awareness of surrounding objects to be avoided and all the time you remained calm and in control.

It was only afterwards that your legs began to shake, your heart pounded, your breathing became short and shallow and you started to sweat. In this way the body released unwanted excess energy and returned to normality.

Whenever our survival is threatened or there is a need for intense activity, we hand over to our automatic pilot, the instincts, whose skills far exceed any we could develop through our conscious mind.

The talents of this pilot have been tested and refined over millions of years of human experience and are fast, efficient and focused on one purpose: to bring the body to a state of perfect readiness as quickly as possible.

In fact, the physical response is the same whether you are running from a lion or having sex!

Your body as a faithful friend only hears the message:

"Prepare for total activity now!"

It is only the conscious mind which is able to appreciate the underlying reason for this degree of activity.

"I am enjoying this, therefore it must be sex!"

(Sex is of course a survival issue, survival of the species).

Any action should be followed by a period of relaxation. However, some people live in a permanent state of readiness, driven sometimes by passion and excitement but more often by fear and insecurity.

When the body is given no time to rest it starts to show signs of hyperactivity where the incoming energy is insufficient to meet demands. Illnesses such as hypertension, stomach ulcers, diabetes, angina, migraines and asthma can reflect this imbalance along with muscle aching, thirst and sweating.

In order to redress the balance we need to emulate the cat. Whilst it is stalking its prey it adopts a state of intense readiness, but when the chase is over it retires for a well deserved rest.

This release of pent up energy, whether by relaxation or expression, is essential so that mind and body can regain their equilibrium. However, in extremely frightening situations, some individuals fail to experience this release, with the *spring* maintaining its heightened tension.

This leads to the condition known as "post traumatic stress syndrome" which is now recognised as a consequence of major disasters, wars or being witness to a terrifying incident.

The closing down of the emotions around a shocking experience is also a survival mechanism, not logically planned but the means by which the mind blanks out something which is too awful to comprehend.

Here the instincts are protecting the integrity of the individual where the threat comes not from outside but from within, ie. instability of the mind could compromise survival of the individual.

As the threat subsides the mind slowly begins to discharge the stored emotions, chemicals and thoughts in order that they can be processed and released.

There is nothing which occurs in our life which, given enough time, space and support, we cannot deal with and release from our being. However, too often, traumatic events are pushed into a corner for fear of upsetting others or in the mistaken belief that the individuals themselves cannot face the ordeal.

New psychological techniques move beyond pity and protection of feelings, recognising that within everyone is an inner strength which will manage the event in its own unique way.

The instincts operate through the autonomic nervous system which is our in-built survival mechanism, acting from what is known as the old or reptilian brain. It consists of two parts, the sympathetic and parasympathetic nervous system, the former relating to alertness and activity and the latter to rest and recuperation. This system by-passes the clever neocortex which deals with logic and also the limbic system which relates to the emotions.

It is now becoming clear that there is a strong link between the pineal gland which is activated by inspiration and intuition and the hypothalamus which is the seat of the sympathetic nervous system. This suggests that the instincts are not only triggered in response to protecting the animal body but also to protecting the soul, which is our link with the eternal source of our being.

Diagram 32

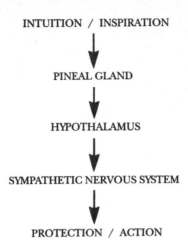

INTUITION / INSPIRATION

↓

PINEAL GLAND

↓

HYPOTHALAMUS

↓

SYMPATHETIC NERVOUS SYSTEM

↓

PROTECTION / ACTION

This link between the instincts and the higher self was highlighted in the *third root race* of man's evolution, when the *Lemurian* Civilisation flourished in a land now covered by the Pacific Ocean. These people were highly attuned to the Will of their Creator and lived in relative harmony with the other Nature Kingdoms in what was known as "the Garden of Eden".

Their end came as man's desire to explore and possess his environment banished him from the Garden until he was ready to surrender his personal desires in the name of Truth and Love.

The instincts enter the energy system through the base chakra stimulating the adrenal glands to produce adrenaline and cortisone which help us to deal with the inevitable stresses of life.

In the animal kingdom the main purpose of instinct is survival of the species where the group is more important than the individual.

Man has evolved beyond this point, developing self-consciousness where ideally each person has free will to think for themselves and act in accord with what they believe to be in the best interests of the species and the planet.

However, too often it means "each person for themself" with little consideration for the greater good.

Until this present time, the continuation of the human race has not been threatened which leads us to believe that we are a superior species with no natural contenders.

I wonder how we would react if we actually acknowledged the presence of other cultures within our Universe. Would this unify our energies or would we find it difficult to accept that such beings came in peace when so much of our planet is still at war?

Until we reconnect to the source of our being and to our own soul energies, recognising that survival of our essence is guaranteed, we will tend to focus all our instinctual energies on that which we believe will provide personal security and continuity.

Such focus is usually based on the world of matter and emotions and includes a statement which says:

"I will survive as long as I have:
Money
A job (even if I hate it)
A purpose or goal
A partner, parent or children to love
People to look after me
A home
An identity (even if this is based on being ill)
A personality which other people admire or need
Pain or suffering
Good looks
Good health
Clear thinking"

Those who think this way usually believe that life is about survival and live in the fear of loss. They apply all their energy to fighting anything or anybody which threatens this security, based on a misunderstanding that these people, objects and identity ever belonged to them in the first place.

Many people would rather die than lose their image or identity.

Example:

Audrey came to see me, concerned that she was developing Alzheimer's disease, having nursed her mother with the same illness for many years.

On enquiring about her life-style, she told me than she and her husband lived in a large house which contained many valuable objects passed down through the families. However, because of the need to secure these objects, the family rarely went away and she could not appreciate them for fear of theft.

Other than her home and looking after her mother her life was empty and she actually worried what would happen when her mother died and she lost the identity of carer.

Audrey's survival was based on material possessions and caring for her mother, neither of which could guarantee her long-term security. Without something more meaningful in her life, there was a good chance that her fear of Alzheimer's disease would manifest. Fortunately, she had the insight to recognise the problem and start to look within for something which would provide greater meaning and security to her life.

Everybody has the right to decide on their own path, although we may receive gentle hints, especially from our body and emotions, that we are out of balance. Despite this, it is still our choice to move the "rudder" to a different direction or to remain on the same course.

Does your survival depend on a particular person or set of circumstances?

Examples:

"I couldn't survive if my husband died"
"I don't know what I would do if I didn't have the children"
"I would rather die than lose my job".
"I could not live without my partner"
"I'd die if I got ill!" (That's asking for trouble!)
"I'd be lost without this friend"
"When the children leave home they will remove my purpose for living".
"I'd rather die than give up my image".
"I'd go mad if I couldn't think straight!"

These are powerful fear-based statements, sending messages out into the ether which will definitely act as an attracting force, bringing towards you that which you most wish to avoid.

This is not because there is some mean old God who thinks that you should suffer but rather that you are the creator of your reality and what you believe or think, happens.

And when it does happen, surprise, surprise, you survive. It is not easy and you often experience pain and suffering. But in the end, if you have the courage to move forward and out of the "doorway" of emotions, you are far wiser after the event.

As you taste the sweet nectar of freedom you realise that the person/object which you believed essential for life had in fact become an albatross around your neck.

A few people choose death at this time for the experience they fear overwhelms their life force. But most people live on, often dramatically changing their survival values, having come to realise that despite being faced with the very thing that they feared most, somehow they were able to reach inside and find the strength, courage and tools to deal with the challenge and come through the other side.

We are never presented with any situation without also being given the tools to deal with it
. . . . . although we are often asked to search deep within ourselves to find them.

You will never know how you will deal with an experience until you meet it, so don't waste time worrying about it or making false proclamations which you cannot live up to when the event occurs.

So what is survival and why do we work so hard to achieve it?

If we return once again to the animal kingdom we see that they have lived by the law of the jungle for as long as animal life has existed on this planet. The law is not enforced through fear but through total instinctual understanding which recognises that without this law the delicate balance of nature cannot survive. The law includes:

Kill or be killed
Survival of the fittest
Defence of one's territory
Survival of the species

See how these rules often involve surrender or letting go not through weakness but through great courage and instinctual knowledge of the Greater Plan. There are no martyrs, no praise for good deeds but rather a total integration of their being into the essence of the jungle.

Some examples of the way in which this works include:

1) Old or injured animals often offer themselves as prey whilst the rest of the herd moves out of reach.

2) Animals use the power of stillness and surrender when they know they cannot outrun their predator. In some instances the sudden stillness confuses the predator who may leave the hunted creature alone.

3) Animals recognise the importance of food and water for survival and have found ways to share a water hole even though they would not normally be found in the same proximity with other species.

4) Animals have no need to kill or hoard more food than they can eat at one time. They do not fear scarcity for they are totally in tune with the process of their environment.

5) They have no need to gain extra land in order to enhance their status in society for each animal is valued as being essential for the maintenance of the delicate equilibrium.

6) Animals have clearly defined territories which are defended when another creature wanders onto their land. However, even though they may use force to remove the invader from their property the attack is rarely fatal, purely acting as a message which is not forgotten.

7) Many animals will move according to the seasons, knowing the best places for food, mating and for the rearing of their young. They are not frightened to move if the circumstances are not optimal for their existence.

Can you see the great wisdom which lies behind these rules?
And where is man, with his/her animal instincts and highly evolved logic and compassion? On many occasions we appear to have sunk lower than the animals, having little regard for other species or for the land to which we owe our existence.

Because we are out of touch with the rhythm of life and the laws which rule this planet we have allowed this instinctual energy and our insecurity to rule us, leading to greater fear of loss, a need to conquer and possess, a greed beyond our needs, a need to protect whatever the cost, a determination to compete often beyond that which is healthy and a desire to destroy anything which gets in the way.

This shows up in the gross imbalances which exist between those who have and those who have not and in the way that the land and seas have been stripped of their goodness in order to satisfy our greed.

And now we have reached a stage when we are being told that our basic needs provided by the planet will do us harm:

"Don't go into the sun without sunscreen"

"Don't drink the water"

"Don't walk outside for fear of pollution from the air"

"The food is unhealthy and lacking in nourishment. Take tablets instead".

"Watch out for the thinning of the ozone layer".

I fully appreciate that much of this advice is valid, but would prefer that we dealt with the cause of the problem rather than just removing ourselves from its presence.

Research

An article which appeared in the British *Lancet* in 1982 showed that the greatest risk of developing malignant melanoma was not in those who permanently sun-bathed. In fact it occurred more commonly in office workers who spent most of their days under lighting which did not include the ultra-violet rays.

Could it be that our sensitivity to the sun's energy is due less to the thinning ozone layer and more to the fact that we now spend so much time inside rather than out in the fresh air?

(V. Beral et al., *"Malignant Melanoma and Exposure to Fluorescent Light at Work,"* Lancet 2 (1982): pp 290–292)

It is time for us to return to our alliance with Nature and, whilst acknowledging the skills and wisdom of the experts, start to listen to our inner hearts and minds.

So let us once again ask the question, who survives? I believe that the instincts can work on two levels:

1) For the survival of the soul, which is the eternal flame which passes from life to life.

2) For the survival of whatever it is that you believe gives you security.

As you can imagine, in the end, whether you are conscious of this or not, the soul will have the last word. If the survival of the individual is compromised by his/her actions then the soul will take us away from the situation.

Unfortunately, when we work from the limited perspective of the emotions or logic we are unable to see this higher reasoning and start to use all our energy to protect that which we fear is being taken away by some unseen enemy.

Look at the words in society associated with illness:

"I conquered cancer" (loud applause)

"I am a cancer survivor"

"She won her battle against cancer"

"I am a victim of AIDS"

"I conquered my over-eating"

This is the language of the jungle. Pure survival. But who is the enemy? The jungle, the body, the cancer?

It is illogical in terms of the law of the jungle for an animal to destroy the very land on which it is dependent for survival. So why would a disease, such as cancer, appear with the prime purpose of destroying its host, the body.

This would only occur for two reasons:

1) If the body was not seen as sacred to survival but that something else, such as an identity within society, was given that powerful position to be protected at all costs even if it meant death of the physical form.

   "She never let anybody down, you could depend on her."

   "She never complained of being sick." (She never complained of anything in her life nor acknowledged her true feelings).

   "She was always happy" (or was it just that she always wore a smile?)

2) If the higher force of the soul decided that the situation was no longer enhancing growth and that fear of change was paralysing the individual.

Cancer is not the enemy; it is a response to an imbalance within the homoeostasis of the individual and rarely due to problems in the physical body. The cancer cells represent a freeing of the individual from structures, habits and responsibilities which are no longer supporting them.

All illness acts as a messenger and provides us with the opportunity for change. Those which ask us to look at life and death issues, such as AIDS, cancer, heart disease are helping us to focus on what is important in life. Often when faced with this question we realise that survival is not about fighting, possessing, owning, conquering but rather about living in harmony with what life presents, striving when we need to strive and resting when it is time to rest.

When we need to use words such as conquer or victim, we are still acting from our animal nature, never understanding that survival is not about fortification, security alarms or vitamin pills but about listening to our intuition and applying the instincts to achieving the optimal reception of our in-dwelling Spirit.

And what is one of the greatest fears, the one to be avoided at all costs? Death! People spend much time and money on trying to escape the only thing which is guaranteed from birth.

Talk about wasted instinctual energies. When death is the enemy, I know who will win!

I believe that the fear of physical death often conceals an even greater anxiety which is the fear of the death of the personality which some people describe as "fear of the void or annihilation".

This is the final surrender to the Will of the Creator so that we can work fully in service to the Universe. However, as there are no vacuums in life, when the space is made, it will be filled, turning what threatened to be annihilation into joy.

Other people have the problem in reverse. They don't fear death, they fear life. These people seek out all sorts of dangerous sports and activities, tempting death, while all the time are fearful of committing to life.

We need to understand that the soul is the only part of us which survives and its energy is enhanced by being free to act from the position of inspiration and intuition and is diminished by the emotion of fear.

When we let go of the need to compete with others and start to recognise our uniqueness then we can live in harmony with our fellow travellers, respecting the law of the jungle, honouring the needs of others and freeing ourselves to experience life to our greatest potential.

EXERCISES TO USE THE INSTINCTS WITH WISDOM
1) When an Exciting Challenge becomes Stressful
We all need challenges in our life. For some, the challenge is getting out of bed in the morning and for others it is scaling a steep and difficult rock face.

Through this process we are stretched and often surprise ourselves as to the strength and fortitude we possess.

But in all things there is a time of stretching and a time of strain, a time when we are firing on all cylinders and a time when the energy starts to fail and illness becomes more prevalent.

Diagram 33

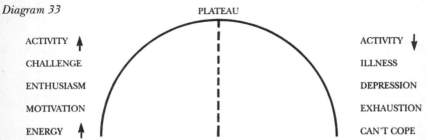

Most of us recognise this moment of shift not through our logical mind but through the bodily signs as the instincts start to appreciate the threat to survival. These symptoms include:

Sweating, worse before and during an event
Anxiety and panic attacks
Trembling (visible or just internal)
Palpitations (fast heart beat)
Missed beats of the heart (the "heart jumps")
Fast, shallow breathing. Wheezing
Shortage of breath when exercising
Sleep disturbance with early morning waking and an over-active mind
Exhaustion on waking and sluggishness on rising
Headaches, especially towards the end of the day
Dry mouth, indigestion, constipation or diarrhoea
Urge to pass water frequently
Increased irritability, weeping or moodiness
Feeling of nausea in difficult situations

Maybe you recognise your own symptoms; they are there as a messenger and a friend. Listen and act.

When you feel such instinctual warnings find a way of reducing the pressure on yourself immediately.

This may include:

1) Changing your posture by perhaps sitting up, walking around the room or changing seats, all of which alter the dynamics of the environment.

2) Speaking if you've been quiet, allowing others to hear how you feel or your own personal opinions.

3) Bringing humour to the situation, changing the atmosphere without necessarily losing respect for either party.

4) Altering your breathing patterns, as described in the chapter on Inspiration, taking longer, deeper breaths into the abdomen; changing posture also facilitates breathing.

5) Allowing a period of stillness and quiet. Take 10 deep breaths and focus on the relationship between the souls present and less on the need to succeed or score.

6) If standing, gently bend your knees, shifting your centre of gravity to the energy centre called the Hara or sacral chakra which is situated around the navel.
   If this does nothing else, it confuses the people around you and brings humour to the situation!

7) Starting to sing, whistle, hum and even dance. Again this confuses others and changes the energy of your breathing, posture and thought patterns. It also gives you space and time to listen to your higher wisdom.

Purely concentrating on the symptoms will only intensify them. Hoping they will just go away rarely works as the instincts are not provided with any reassurance that the mind is actively dealing with the threat to survival. Only by removing the pressure from the fight and flight scenario, will the threat subside.

2) Develop an Inner Security

Sit or lie in quiet meditation and imagine yourself as a tree.

The trunk of the tree is the body. Feel the strength of this trunk as it gently sways in the wind.

Look at the rings of wisdom within the trunk, showing you just how far you have come.

See a rich energy running up and down the inside of the trunk providing nourishment to the whole tree.

Now see the roots emerging from your feet. They go in all directions; some to the side to provide stability and some deep down to provide attachment. The earth is rich and nurturing and you feel yourself being lovingly contained.

Move your vision to see the branches, recognising that they grow in all directions and are rich in life as they stretch towards the sun.

Your tree is securely held between the Father Sky and the Mother Earth, your spiritual parents. Allow yourself to feel their energy move up and down the trunk providing inner strength and a sense of belonging.

Whenever you feel uncertain, return to the security experienced within this exercise and you will receive inner strength. Through the tree we link our Earth life with that of the Spirit world. The roots are our instincts, whilst the branches represent our yearning for inspiration.

3) Learning to Let Go

Throughout the text, I have suggested that, if our survival and security are totally dependent on other people or objects, we may run into problems.

Whilst I am not asking you to move away from these people, I do suggest that you learn to recognise that you, as a soul, will survive whatever happens, and within this thought there is security. Every talent, relationship and possession is a gift to be enjoyed and appreciated but they are not your identity.

Remember those times when you lost someone or something without which you thought you could not survive. And yet, here you are. Where did that strength come from? Possibly from the love and support of others, possibly from the inner encouragement from the one who passed over. Could it have also arisen from your own inner courage and determination to find out who you really are?

Trust that inner strength and let it guide you!

> *"If you realize that all things change,
> there is nothing you will try to hold on to.
> If you aren't afraid of dying,
> there is nothing you can't achieve."*
>
> (Tao Te Ching, Lao-tzu)

Chapter 8

The Mirror

The purpose of life is to interact with our environment in such a way that we reach a state of wholeness and enlightenment whilst at the same time adding to the Universal Consciousness by releasing the energy which has been generated.

To achieve this result we project impulses from the various levels of consciousness onto the Mirror of Existence (the world) which acts as the vessel for this dynamic experience.

As our desires, emotions and dramas become reality the truth of who we are is revealed not only to those around us but also to ourselves.

As we act so are we known.

Whether we acknowledge this creative power and its reflection is dependent on the scope of our perception, for we can only see what we believe. Many would be pleasantly surprised to discover their true identity once they looked beyond their limited range of vision and saw the radiant light-being who is just waiting to be noticed.

One reason we are unable to recognise our own creations is that we say one thing and think another:

"I really want to start my own business".

My subconscious says:

"It will never work, I've never succeeded at anything".

Guess what, the venture fails and with a sigh we conclude:

"I try to create my own reality but it never works for me!"

At other times we are motivated to act in accordance with the desires of our ego, ignoring our intuition which may be saying "Wait!" When plans fail to reach fruition we feel frustrated but a wise person will sit back and hear the inner voice say:

"The time has not yet come".

So much energy would be saved if our thoughts were clear and we focused only on those messages which come from the highest levels of awareness such as the intuition or inspiration.

To understand the process which leads us towards wholeness we need to recognise the different roles played by the Mirror and how certain stages have evolved whilst others still require refinement.

THE PROJECTED IMPULSE

The impulse which is projected onto the mirror is dependent on the dominant level of awareness from which the individual is acting be it instinctual, emotional, logical, intuitive or inspirational.

The primary outlet for this creative spark, independent of the source, is through the eyes. We literally project into our world that which we wish to see.

In this way, the eyes can no longer be seen as a purely sensory organ gathering information from the outside world, but as also possessing a motor function which has the ability to send forth impulses from the deeper recesses of the mind.

Ancient cultures have always appreciated this dual nature with reference to "the evil eye" where it was believed that certain individuals had the power to do harm just by looking at you. Shamanic teaching used the expressive function of the eye to project a thought into the environment so that students could not only hear the message but also be part of it.

Today's "virtual reality" created by computers simulates this very concept perhaps allowing us to start to appreciate what the older civilisations have always known.

The eyes are the window of the soul.

The impulse travels to the eyes via the chakra which is specific to that particular function of the mind. So that in the case of emotions it is the solar plexus which is most active during this process. (Diagram 34)

For thousands of years this was the dominant chakra and many were blinded by its "sun-like" qualities failing to look beyond their own desires in terms of purpose and achievement. The heart and crown chakras had little influence leaving the individual devoid of the wisdom and compassion which emanates from the Higher Self.

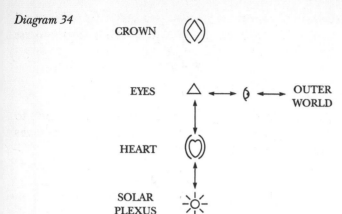

Diagram 34

CROWN

EYES — — OUTER WORLD

HEART

SOLAR PLEXUS

With the expansion of logic, expressed through the throat chakra, the "mirage" produced by the solar plexus has started to fade, encouraging mankind to turn its eyes upwards towards a Greater Light.

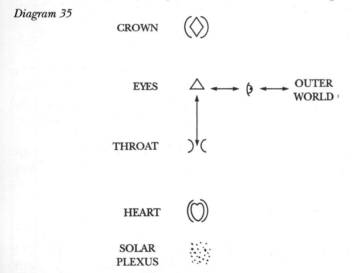

Diagram 35

CROWN

EYES — — OUTER WORLD

THROAT

HEART

SOLAR PLEXUS

We are now ready to take the next step, realigning our heart, third eye and crown chakras and thereby allowing intuition and inspiration to guide us towards our spiritual destiny.

The pineal gland linked to the crown chakra will then be fully active, functioning as a crystal prism to focus the incoming energy from the Higher Self towards the third eye.

Here some of the impulse will pass out through the *cones* of the physical eyes into the outside world and act as an attracting force for the manifestation of form. The remainder of the energy will travel down to the heart chakra where its essence will be matched against the inner truth of the individual for, without the approval of the intuition, the idea can go no further.

Diagram 36

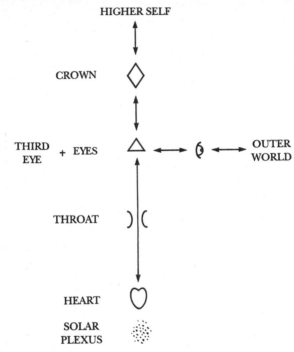

Following the creation of form, the reflection will be projected back through the retina of the eyes and then along the path of the outgoing message until it is matched against the original idea. If there is harmony, then the soul's vibration will expand; if not, the impulse will be sent out again until a mirror image is produced.

At this exciting period in our evolution many people around the world are working to link heart and head so that major decisions which will affect the future of our planet come from a place of love and wisdom rather than from analysis and pure logic.

SEEING OUR OWN REFLECTION

When the expressed impulse meets the physical world whether this is our body or our surroundings, it attracts towards itself that which will transform thought into reality.

Diagram 37

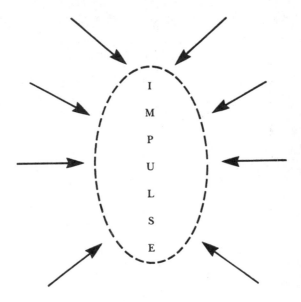

I
M
P
U
L
S
E

MANIFESTATION

The specific quality of this creation comes from the ever-changing time/space dynamic and from the fact that we function from many different levels of consciousness at any one time. Diversity within a common framework is the essence of evolution here on Earth for, as each person strives towards wholeness, their unique interaction with the world adds to the wealth of possibilities within the Universal Mind.

Children are taught little about their individuality and are encouraged to compete in, and adapt to, the social structure. In this way many adults fail to reach soul fulfilment, never revealing their true strengths and are destined to remain in the shadows of mediocrity.

In order to reach wholeness we attract towards us that which reflects those parts of ourselves which are still masked. By recognising and acknowledging these aspects we can then integrate them into our being through the power of love, including those parts which we had previously found unacceptable.

Only through love without conditions can we become whole.

We can choose to ignore these gifts of truth but as we tune into the intuition we find that the soul's gentle persuasion opens our eyes to what is
important.

There are three main areas where we can see ourselves clearly within the
mirror:

1) Through the world of form especially in our job, hobbies, interests or
   home.
2) Through other people.
3) In our body – particularly when we become ill.

REFLECTIONS IN THE WORLD OF FORM

"All the world's a stage . . . ."

It is easy to recognise ourselves in achievements which began as a dream
or idea and which provided us with a tremendous sense of pride. It is far
more difficult to acknowledge situations we have produced subconsciously
and which are just as relevant.

Energy follows thought but not always in the way we planned.

Examples:

1) *A man wished every night for a Rolls-Royce car.*
   *Then, one morning, a driver lost control of his vehicle and it plunged through the
   front wall of the home of the man with the dreams.*
   The Rolls-Royce had arrived but not in the anticipated manner!

Be careful how you express your dreams for they will come true!

At other times we may be drawn to something within our environment
which contains a message beneficial to our inner growth.

2) *A friend was complaining about litter in the countryside.*
   *As she finished talking she dropped her cigarette end onto the ground, stamped it
   out and without another thought walked away.*

If something or somebody attracts our attention we are being offered a personal reflection; in this case: "Where do I create litter and pollution; is it
through my thoughts or actions?"

Sometimes it is the media which provides the reflection.

3) *"Whenever the television shows the suffering of children or animals I start to weep".*

Children and animals represent innocence and when they suffer we feel their helplessness in a world where there is no room for those without a voice. There would be few people not affected by this media coverage but some feel it deeply, revealing an inner child who is lost and powerless desperately crying out for love and attention.

The media helps us to ask the question:

Where am I starving?
Where is my poverty if it is not material?
Where am I neglected or unloved?

By healing the areas in our own life which require urgent consideration we can then be of greater service to others because our own needs are being met.

REFLECTIONS THROUGH OTHER PEOPLE

"Mirror, mirror on the wall, who is the fairest of them all?"

As social beings we are constantly connecting and disconnecting from our fellow man some of whom we meet only briefly whilst others are with us for life.

All relationships will have an effect upon us to a lesser or greater extent, depending on the amount of spiritual and emotional energy generated at that time.

Our family (chosen prior to incarnation) will usually be our greatest teachers subtly projecting us towards wholeness even though they may be unaware of their influence. Those whom we attract as partners, friends and spouses provide us with loving support as well as bringing with them some part of ourselves which we may not at first recognise.

By committing to the relationship both parties have the opportunity to grow although this may not always occur at the same rate or in the same direction. At some point it may be necessary to change the format of the partnership and this will require honest communication and unconditional love.

The people we attract come in many forms, each with their own unique contribution.

Soul Group

You may remember an occasion when you met someone apparently for the first time and yet it was as if you were connecting with a long-lost friend. Soul group relationships are often brief but profound, providing help, direction, love and support outside the emotional ties of the family and close friends.

Example:

I had just finished a long-term relationship and was feeling sad and empty. To distract my thoughts, I wandered into a bookshop and started to browse.
As I leant forward to take a book from the shelf someone else reached for it first. I turned to face the culprit and found myself staring into the eyes of an old "soul friend".
There was no need for introductions and four hours later we parted having spent a wonderful afternoon talking and supporting each other in a way that is only possible with those from your soul group.
As is often the case, we never saw each other again and yet that meeting helped me to see life in a totally new light.

Perhaps you can recall a similar situation and know the pleasure of meeting someone who loves and honours you whilst also reminding you of your true essence. They bring with them a gift from God and may appear in the most unusual places. It is not important to maintain contact, for the healing which occurs at that moment is instantaneous and works at the deepest soul level.

Those who Inspire

There are those people we attract whom we greatly admire and respect for their manner, talents or achievements. Our appreciation is often enhanced by a subtle recognition of part of ourselves within their performance.

Role models are a powerful way of reaching wholeness as long as we do not afford these individuals guru-like status and fail to acknowledge our own amazing path. Their task is to bring to light hidden potential and then allow their admirers to adopt their own unique style.

Comfortable Similarities

Certain friends or family members have a special place in our heart, creating a relationship which is usually symbiotic with each contributing something of value and committed to making it work. These people reflect aspects of our being which we know and love whilst we return the compliment without conditions.

If you feel that there are very few people in your life who fit into this category, it is important to ask: *"Do I love and value myself?"* When we hold ourselves in poor regard then we will only see and meet those who reinforce the beliefs which maintain the negative illusion.

A thousand people may tell you that you have an inner beauty, but if you don't embrace this belief you will disregard their comments and, in doing so, turn your back on them. Could it be that all these people are wrong because you are always right or is it possible that you need to review your values?

The way forward is to open your heart and mind to the new images, allowing the intuition to guide you towards the light of your being.

Finding Parts Hidden in the Shadows

Finally, we will attract towards us individuals with whom there appears to be no obvious connection and yet through our emotional body we recognise, often unconsciously, that they are here to teach us something.

"Sorry! What on earth could that ignorant slob ever teach me?"

(Well, compassion for your fellow man would be a start!)

What we dislike in others is usually present in ourselves. What a thought!

The link is not always obvious and is often linked to the cause rather than the effect.

Example:

You don't approve of your friend's drinking habit and remark: "I'd never do that". But alcohol is the means by which your friend enhances their confidence. You are unable to condone their habit but, because you are also shy, you can now sympathise with their problem and start to accept the similarities between you.

Time and time again we attract towards us the same type of individual and fail to recognise the connection and our own reflection in the mirror. When the message is eventually heard we look back and see a pattern which has been repeated throughout our life, often accompanied by pain and frustration.

If we take time to understand other people from their perspective we can start to understand ourselves.

"Walk a mile in someone else's moccasins before you judge them."

Examples:

1) "My wife becomes irritable and demanding when she is overworked and will not ask for help."

(You are also a perfectionist who prefers to do a job yourself rather than delegate. When you are under pressure, instead of becoming irritated, you switch off and go to sleep leaving your wife to cope alone.)

2) "But he is so dull and boring, just wanting to sit and talk while I need constant excitement in my life".

(Your criticism of his ability to be still may be an attempt to block out your own inner voice which urges you to follow his example.)

3) *"She comes into the office, never offers to take on extra work, has an hour for lunch and then goes home at five while I am slaving away at the typewriter, answering all the calls, never stopping for lunch and leaving late!"*

(Who's got the problem? Your aggravation denotes a degree of envy of someone who is not a slave to their work and who knows how to set boundaries. Perhaps it is time to assess priorities and create balance in your life.)

4) *"Well, that's fine but there is no possible connection between me and my domineering mother-in-law!"*

(Domination comes from a sense of insecurity, leading to the need to control one's environment. Your means of control may be expressed differently through criticism or aloofness but the message is the same.)

5) *"I can't trust him, he never tells the truth".*

(Do you? Are you always honest with yourself and others? Do you ever say one thing whilst thinking another in order to keep the peace or so that other people are not hurt by your comments? Maybe a truthful remark expressed with compassion is kinder than a deliberate lie designed to keep the peace.)

6) *"He's so lazy. I just wish he would do something useful".*

(There are very few truly lazy people; most individuals who exhibit this quality are surrounded by fear of failure or of success, intensified by other people's pressure to move. Those who hassle need to stand back and recognise that the person who fears change or failure is often themselves. It is very comfortable to project one's own problems onto others, creating stagnation not only in your own life but in those you wish to help.)

7) *"He's such an extrovert, he just doesn't care what people think. Sometimes I don't know where to look".*

(Maybe there is a part of you longing to express itself fully without being so sensitive to the opinions of others.)

8) *"Since the separation, one child throws temper tantrums whilst the other cries all the time. Me? I just get on with life, what else is there to do?"*

(Children easily pick up the mood of their parents, even though nothing is said, becoming surrogate emotional characters when the adults are unable to express their own true feelings. Treating the child alone does not treat the cause.)

9) *"People always seem to be angry with me".*

(Anger attracts anger especially if the feeling has been buried for some time. If we find ourselves repeatedly surrounded by specific emotions we need to ask where is the emotion within us and start to express it appropriately.)

10) *"I was so upset when a friend told me about the death of her sister and I didn't even know her!"*

(Chance comments or stories tap into our own memory and reveal something hidden in the shadows which requires healing.)

Look at aspects in other people which irritate you or make you feel uncomfortable. Now be honest, is there not a correlation between yourself and these people with your own characteristics waiting to be acknowledged?

If the answer is "yes", why walk around incomplete when enlightenment is calling out to you? Make friends with all parts of your being, freeing yourself to enjoy and experience the richness of life.

REFLECTIONS THROUGH THE PHYSICAL BODY

The body, like the outer world, acts as a vehicle for the manifestation of Spirit into Matter. It reflects our moods, thoughts, feelings and inner essence, faithfully reproducing them in the day-to-day function of the cells of our body.

Disease represents both a crisis and an opportunity for change, offering clear guide-lines as to the new direction to be taken. These indicators may appear as the symptoms of the disease, the pathology of the affected organ or the language used by the patient to describe their condition especially when the intensity of feeling does not equate to reality.

Examples:
1) *"My heart is no longer in my job"*, said the man who had just suffered his first heart attack.

2) *"I feel as if I've entered a cul-de-sac and can't get out"*, reported the business man whose coronary arteries are narrowing, causing him to complain of angina.

3) *"When I'm around her, I just can't breathe. She never lets me get a word in edge-ways"*. Not surprisingly this patient has asthma.

4) *"My period pains incapacitate me. They are so inconvenient"*, states a woman who has climbed the corporate ladder and is competing fiercely with the men in her company.

5) *"I have such terrible lower back pain and there is no-one to help me"*. The spine represents structure and those with lower back problems often feel unsupported.

6) *"My shoulders are aching as if I am carrying a heavy load"*, complains the woman who feels responsible for everybody, including the problems of the world!

7) *"My stomach is tied up in knots; I'm so worried"* frets the young man who has taken on so much work that he feels overwhelmed. His stomach reflects the need to divide his work into more manageable segments so that the processes of digestion and absorption can be eased.

Our body is our best friend, willing to go many miles with us and yet also willing to be objective "pulling the plug" on our activities if it feels that we are no longer walking on our own soul path.

There is a more detailed account of the psycho-spiritual message of disease in my book *Frontiers of Health*.

THE CREATIVE ENERGY

Having united impulse and reality it is important to be able to release the created form or energy so that it can become a creator in its own right. Unfortunately, due to our obsession with the world of matter, we tend to believe that once we have produced something it belongs to us, failing to understand that energy must flow so that we are ready for the next encounter.

Analogy

You bake a cake and, instead of enjoying it, you place it on the table as the centre piece of your life. Each day you change the cloth under the plate but you never eat a single crumb for you want your masterpiece to remain perfect.

As the days pass, the cake turns mouldy and you become sad. In the end nobody enjoys the wonderful taste of the cake even though this was the only true purpose of its creation.

Trapped or stagnant energy eventually turns against those who try to contain it, calling upon the instinctual impulse to free it either through fight or by surrender, occasionally leading to death of the physical form.

Non-attached creativity leads to harmonic flow and contentment.

By learning to enjoy and participate fully in every moment of our life without becoming dependent on any object, person or identity, we free ourselves for guidance in the direction which will allow us to reach our full potential.

So:

The energy of money needs to flow, providing growth and investment not only for the individual but for the Greater Good

Gifts and talents must be shared so that they may touch the hearts of many

Children require encouragement to "fly on their own" in order to continue the cycle of life

Friendships need space to breathe so that new impulses can enrich them

Ideas, like seeds, require nourishment and varied conditions in order to grow and blossom

Knowledge is useless unless combined with wisdom and love and used in the service of mankind.

I recommend that you review your own life and see where you are holding onto old creations which may appear as:

Outdated beliefs

Relationships which have little or nothing in common

Books lying on shelves unread and gathering dust

Momentoes stored in the attic, never reviewed or enjoyed

Cupboards packed with items which one day "may be useful"

Notebooks filled with information from lectures and workshops but never re-read

Half-finished jobs waiting for the "right time" for completion

Dreams and aspirations destined to stay in the land of fantasy as there is no space for them to become reality.

Imagine a day when you can live fully in the world and yet be totally aware of your spiritual connections.

Imagine a day when you can enjoy all the glorious gifts of God without being dependent upon them for your existence.

Imagine a day when you can embrace each new experience as an exciting challenge without fear of failure or disappointment.

This is not a dream; when we step freely into the mirror of existence, trusting our inner guidance to lead us towards greater joy, service and fulfilment, it will become reality.

Chapter 9

Illusions

The mirror faithfully reproduces the impulses which emerge from our belief system, and provides us with order, objectivity and structure. However, we are sometimes dependent upon a conviction which no longer supports soul growth and cannot be endorsed by our intuition. This leads to the appearance of illusions within the mirror – an illusion being "a sensuous perception of an external object involving a false belief" (Concise Oxford Dictionary).

The present social structure reinforces this trick of vision encouraging us to accept what others say (especially those in authority), so that we give away our power without a second thought. Indeed, in civilisations where technology dominates, the ability to think for oneself is being eroded by an increased reliance on computers to guide every step we take.

I cannot believe that this is a healthy phase in our evolution for we will reach a stage where those who control the computers and media will control the world. Unless those individuals operate from a position of wisdom and compassion, it will be essential for each person to tune into their own higher wisdom and accept only that which resonates with the Universal Truth.

Illusions can be personal, familial, cultural or planetary, with the "majority" usually deciding what is reality and what is fantasy based on logical analysis, research and knowledge passed down through the ages.

Go back in time to when we believed that the world was flat and those who said otherwise were seen as liars, heretics or insane. In retrospect which was the illusion? Any belief must be able to stand up to scrutiny and be sufficiently flexible to embrace new information whatever the source.

Present day debates include the existence of UFOs with as many advocates as sceptics although I believe the time is now ripe to bring the truth into the open. The wind of change which we are experiencing upon this Earth is transforming a considerable number of traditional structures, clearing a path for new patterns of thinking.

Today, many are starting to question their sense of values, seeing for the first time that what appeared to be solid and real was in fact an illusion, a shadow which disappeared when the Light was overhead.

Here are some examples of current illusions heard at various seminars which I am sure reflect a common theme:

1) "If only they would change everything would be alright".

How easily we forget that we can't change anybody else, we can only change ourselves. Some think that if they keep nagging then perhaps one day they will be heard as if the message wasn't clear enough on the first occasion.

And have you noticed that the more you are nagged the less you want to change? We expend endless energy in the name of love, believing that we know what is best for other people.

"I'm doing it for their own good. I know they have the potential to be more than they are now", (and as Lionel Fyfield says, *"I love the potential more than the person!"*)

We apply our own set of values, invading the private sanctuary of those we believe need help without ever asking: *"What can I do to love and support you more?"*

This form of spiritual arrogance is one of the most difficult lessons to learn especially when we see those we love walk a path which is different from the one we would have chosen. We may see it as our duty to put them on "the right track" ignoring their judgment in matters of their own life.

True love suggests that we let them know our concerns, offer loving support and then stand back showing them that we trust their higher wisdom.

At this point we may realise that they are never going to change and we can experience grief as our *fantasy* dies and we acknowledge that we have never really loved the person, only our dreams. Once we face the truth, a truly honest and loving relationship can develop.

2) "I'm on a Spiritual Path, but I'm not very far along".

Everybody is on a journey of discovery, each unique and tailor-made for the individual. However, in a world where competition is rife, there is a tendency to compare our spiritual growth with others failing to recognise the complexity of the situation.

This then encourages those with poor self-esteem to believe that their path is long and never ending and they are just at the start.

"One day I'll be better/kinder/wiser/more enlightened but I'm not there yet". This

illusion is often confirmed by those who are only too happy to take advantage of individuals with poor self-worth in order to expand their own ego.

I see that the *vertical* managerial ladder has been replaced by the *horizontal* spiritual path, walked by those who never believe they are "good enough". These individuals complete one task but when congratulated will respond: *"Yes, that's okay but I'll do better next time!"*

It is important to recognise our beauty and perfection now and celebrate personal achievements rather than constantly look to the future for happiness.

Be content to stand still and become the hub of your own wheel of life.

3) "Change takes time".

Change takes as long as you believe it will take!

"Well healing won't happen overnight".
"Why not? Did the Master Healers of the past suggest that twenty sessions were needed before a cure could occur?"

No, it is faith which heals and manifests wholeness; faith in those who facilitate the process but more importantly faith in our own healing ability. True miracles reveal an almost instantaneous metamorphosis involving every aspect of the individual from cell nucleus to Universal Consciousness.

Time is the illusion; it is as long or short as we need it to be. It is how we use the time which is important, remembering that we are already whole and it is within our power to allow the enlightened being within to shine forth in the service of mankind.

4) "Guilt is essential for life"
It is easy to live one's life burdened by the energy of guilt:
"If only I had acted differently/been there/thought it through then it wouldn't have happened".

We have all done things which afterwards we wished we hadn't but the only purpose of such insight is to attempt to put right the wrongs, choose to act differently next time and to ask for forgiveness both from ourselves and from others.

For some, their expression of guilt is a way of showing love which is a sad reflection on the state of the relationship. Long-term guilt creates stagnation and in the end changes little except that we now have an excuse for failing to live life fully.

Perhaps it is time to convert the lessons of the past into action for the future, recognising that there is no such thing as a mistake only opportunities to grow.

5) "Spirituality equals poverty"

On the contrary, the more we are in tune with our spiritual roots the greater the wealth we experience in all areas of our life, though it is not uncommon to find that the material world then holds less attraction as we encounter richness in love, fulfilment, service, joy and contentment.

It is not essential to give up everything we own in order to reach enlightenment but rather to let go of our attachment to the worlds of matter, emotions and logic so that we can experience true spiritual abundance.

6) "People need me"

I have seen many people surrounded by problems which they themselves have created in order to avoid stepping into the mirror of existence:

"I'd love to, but . . . . . "

"What are you going to do when there are no further problems?" I venture.

"Oh, that will never happen, they are so dependent on me!"

Who is dependent on whom?

Could it be that we contribute in some way to other peoples' difficulties by our fear of change? I have seen tremendous healing take place when one member of the family has the courage to follow their intuition and take the next step on their path knowing that in this way they are offering true love to their family.

7) "I'd love to do something but I have so many things to sort out first".

It is easy to become fixated by a small, yet demanding area of our life, failing to stand back and see the wider picture. When we are in the mud, however much we stir it up and stamp our feet, we are still in the mud. It is only when we have the courage and conviction to step onto firmer land we see that this area of turmoil is, indeed, only a puddle.

Don't allow this life's experiences to over-shadow the wealth of knowledge and wisdom that is available to you from your eternal soul consciousness. Stand in the Light and things will start to fall into place.

8) Illusions concerning Love

In every culture there are books, verses and songs dedicated to the power of love, which is essential to the soul's existence. But I believe that this sacred word has been used to create illusions, many of which are not beneficial to the individual and will only lead us further from the truth.

To clear the mist, I suggest that:

a) **Love** *is a state of being not doing. We are in love.*

b) **Love** *is a creative space where anything is allowed to happen.*

c) **Unconditional love** *cannot be given or taken for, in the very act of giving and taking, conditions emerge.*

d) **Love** *cannot be taken away as part of a bribe: "I'll love you if . . . ."; this conditional love is not even worth expressing.*

e) **Love** *is a state of acceptance, without sacrifice or compromise.*
   Sacrifice is giving without the willingness to receive gracefully. Compromise without true communication often leads to denial of one's own inner being in an attempt to maintain an unnatural peace.

f) **Love** *means "doing unto others as you would do unto yourself".*
   Love therefore needs to start with ourselves.

g) **Love** *does not allow secrets, elitism or special favours.*

h) **Love** *is not duty for this involves debts and expectations.*
   Act from respect not duty.

i) **Love** *cannot be bought, nor does it judge or disapprove.*
   It is like the sun which does not discriminate but welcomes all equally into its rays.

j) **Love** *is not pity for this fails to see and honour the beautiful soul within.*

k) **Love** *does not hide behind the fear of hurting others.*

As the Prophet says in the book by *Kahlil Gibran*:

> *"Love gives naught but itself and takes naught but from itself.*
> *Love possesses not nor would it be possessed;*
> *for love is sufficient unto love".*

Chapter 10

Living in the Light

There comes a stage in our journey towards wholeness when we need to adjust our range of vision in order to encompass parts of ourselves which reflect our multi-dimensional nature.

This phase of enlightenment is one of the most exciting times in our life and yet also one of the greatest challenges, for in order to achieve this transformation we must integrate the lower levels of consciousness with those related to our higher self.

In other words, we must surrender our personal will to the Will of God, merge the power of our emotions with the higher power of love and focus our instinctual energy away from personal survival towards creative living.

This phase of initiation can only occur when we are able to recognise ourselves separate from the possessions of the material world, from the emotional power games and from our limiting belief systems.

It is as if by then we are able to stand on a mountain looking down on the world we know and yet at the same time experience a whole new vista. To reach that altitude it is essential to have done extensive training upon the foothills for only then are we able to leave behind the unnecessary aspects of the instincts, emotions and logic and take with us only that which supports the next step of our journey.

Some attempt to climb the mountain before they have experienced themselves within the three-dimensional world and become lost within the mists of illusion which create a veil around the base of the mountain. Eventually, they are forced to return to the valley where, by applying themselves to the events of life, they become better equipped to guide themselves through the semi-darkness finally to emerge into brilliant sunshine.

The path to wholeness is one of self-discovery.
When you think you know who you are it is time to lose yourself to the greater vision.

Such expansion in consciousness involves the alignment of the crown, third eye and heart chakras which when fully functional allow inspiration, intention and intuition to become the guiding forces.

This transition rarely occurs without some objection being raised by our highly developed logic which associates the surrender of personal will with annihilation, powerlessness and loss of control. It employs the power of analysis to produce a myriad of reasons or excuses why things should remain the same, enlisting words and phrases such as:

"Yes, but . . . .".
"What if . . . . .?"
"When . . . happens, then I'll . . . . .".
"It's not that easy!"
"I don't want to hurt others".
"I'm too lazy/poor/stupid/busy/needed etc. . . . . . ."
"But what if it doesn't work?"
"It will probably fail anyway".
"We only grow when life is difficult".
"It's irresponsible to be too carefree".
"It won't happen overnight".
"I feel guilty".
*"But **ho-o-ow**?"*

You may recall a conversation with someone who expresses the desire to change and grow while subconsciously their body and emotions are less enthusiastic. As you offer suggestions, they lead you through a maze of long explanations as to why they **cannot** possibly move even though they requested your advice in the first place.

As they foil each of your recommendations they let out a sigh thinking:

"Phew, she nearly made me change!"

I suggest that rather than continue the charade it is far more beneficial for all concerned to say:

"It sounds as if you are happy to stay where you are; if you change your mind I'm willing to offer my guidance".

Spiritual initiation involves more than just a "pleasant thought" in the head; it requires courage and commitment from the heart and a willingness to step forward, often into the unknown, having faith in the Wisdom of the Universe.

There is **no pressure** from a higher authority for any of us to change or surrender our will. Such methods of control come from the lower mind which has often used words such as "should, must and ought" to drive the individual forward.

When the time is right, we make a voluntary decision to merge our will with that of the Creator without setting conditions, knowing that we are then fulfilling our greater purpose.

This requires a deep faith in oneself which is built upon the foundations of honesty, respect and love.

Some believe that they have reached this stage but even at the point of surrender cannot let go of their need to control:

"I'm frustrated because everything is moving so slowly; I'm impatient to get started".

"I know what's needed and I'm prepared to put my energies into that".

"I have so much to give to the world, I can't understand why I am not being used".

"I'm here to save the world" (even though it is not the world who has the problem!)

"I want to help people as it is easy for me to see what they need". (What about the reflection?)

All these statements suggest that the plan of the individual is more important than that of the Creator. Once we surrender our will, time, place and purpose are no longer in our control. It is then that we need to trust our intuition implicitly, using our logical mind to focus the inspirational impulses which we receive.

Surrender does not mean complacency or sacrifice but rather that we offer our integrity, wisdom and strength to be used in the service of God.

On an emotional level, the threat to personal power, which has usually been maintained through separation rather than connection, leads some to attempt to play "power games" with God, unaware that the greater power of love awaits them:

"I'm working in service to mankind but I will hold back a little bit of my energy (in the name of resentment) so that I never lose myself completely".

"I am willing and ready to step into life trusting the Universal energy but, once in a while, I'll panic and run back under the covers looking for the support and attention I need".

"I have faith in the Greater Plan, but occasionally I will criticise some aspect of it just to show that I still have an opinion".

I have an image that as we clothe ourselves in certain emotions, believing that these make us strong and invincible, our Creator lovingly looks on, seeing children playing with dressing-up clothes, knowing that one day we will be ready to shed these and stand naked in the sight of God.

As someone once said:

"As we hang from the cliff edge waiting to fall into the arms of God, we may release nine fingers but, while one finger remains, we are still holding on".

We do not need to deny our emotions; we should instead use their transformational qualities to enhance the cohesive power of love so that this may motivate all our thoughts and actions.

Instinctively, as we move from a point of living to survive to living to create, we encounter fears generated by years of defending our position.
"Who will I be when I'm not me?"
"What will become my driving force when I am no longer being driven by my personal desires or needs?"
"What would happen if I actually reached my ultimate goal?"
"I am frightened of rejection/failure/success/poverty/the unknown".

These are all reasonable questions or statements, and yet to the soul they are illusions created by a limiting level of consciousness.

The answers lie beyond the questions for it is within the stillness of mind and body that we find the truth; here we learn that it is we who *reject* aspects of ourselves, we who *fail* in our soul's purpose, denying ourselves *success,* we who experience *poverty* of the soul and we who are scared of *knowing* the beautiful and lovable being who is present within.

At the point of transformation the voice of our fears can appear very loud and protesting, creating darkness and disorientation. Yet, when the inner guidance is strong, the disharmonic sounds eventually start to resonate with the inner truth and harmony prevails.

There can be no more power games, no more bargaining and no more promises but only an inner desire to move beyond separation and connect with our own truth and hence to life eternal.

The writing of this book has been a journey of self-discovery initiated by seeing the title, etched in stone, during a dream last year. Time and again I recognised aspects of myself which had been masked or false belief systems which had directed my life. On occasions I felt like *Alice in Wonderland* following what appeared to be a solid lead only to discover the illusion at the end of the tunnel. Sometimes I became so overwhelmed by the complexity of my thoughts that I cast aside the creative impulses, only to wake the following morning with new thoughts and fresh impetus.

As the pieces came together in the jigsaw puzzle, I found that my outer identities and structures became less important as my strength, sense of connection and inner knowing were magnified.

I realised how easy it is to become fixated by a single smudge on the mirror believing that this is who we are and failing to see the beautiful Light Being who fills the rest of the mirror.

I see the time has come for all of us to clean our mirror and step fully into the Light, entering a world where there is an eternal source of power, the potential for total fulfilment and the opportunity to fly with the wings of angels.

Bibliography

Esoteric Healing, Alice Bailey; The Lucis Press
A Treatise on White Magic, Alice Bailey; The Lucis Press
Mutant Message Down Under, Marlo Morgan; Aquarian Press
Feel the Fear and Do It Anyway, Susan Jeffers; Arrow Books
The Celestine Prophecy, James Redfield; Bantam Books
The Prophet, Kahlil Gibran; Heinemann, London
Tao Te Ching, Lao-tzu, translated by Stephen Mitchell; Kyle Cathie

Index

and emotions, 82
exercises, 26–7
problems, 88, 98
burn out, 62

C
calming exercise, 27
cancer, 54, 79, 95, 96
carbon dioxide, 23
catarrh, 55
cerebral hemisperes, 51
chakras, 18, 19, 24, 38–9, 102–4, 122
    ajna, (third eye) 38–9, 103, 104, 122
    base, 90
    crown, 24, 38–9, 46–7, 103, 104, 122
    heart, 37, 38–9, 46–7, 103, 104, 122
    solar plexus, 82, 102–4
    throat, 62, 103, 104
challenges, 97–8
change, 117, 122
    and death, 92–3
    and emotions, 73–4, 81
    and fear, 11, 53, 60
    and relationships, 116
choice, 12–13
compartmentalising, 54–5
competition, 116–17
conformity, 43–4, 58–9
confusion, 63
connection/re-connection, 2, 4, 5–6, 11, 23, 24, 33, 39, 43, 110
consciousness, 3, 10–11
control, 11–12, 76, 123–4
    and emotions, 81
cramps, 54
creativity, 16–17, 112–13
    and logic, 62–3, 65
crown chakra, 24, 38–9, 46–7, 103, 104, 122 *and see* chakras

D
dance, 65, 98
death
    and change, 92–3

fulfilment, 33, 35, 36
fun, 36

G
gall stones, 54
glands
    adrenal, 90
    endocrine, 78
    hypothalamus, 38, 70, 89, 90
    pineal, 24–5, 89, 90, 103
grief, 73–4
growth, 121–3
guilt, 60, 79, 80, 117
gurus, 59–60
gut feelings, 31–2 *and see* intuition

H
happiness, 36
headaches, 62, 98 *and see* migraines
healing/healers, 4, 7–8, 117
heart
    chakra, 37, 38–9, 46–7, 103, 104, 122 *and see* chakras
    disease, 54, 58
    and intuition, 37–40
    and see angina
    missed beats, 98
Higher Self, 33–4 *and see* Soul
honesty, 16, 48, 76
hurt(s), 50, 52, 83–4
hyperactivity, 88
hypersensitivity, 31
hypertension, 88
hypothalamus, 38, 70, 89, 90 *and see* glands
hyperventilation, 54

I
identity, 1–3, 72, 91–3
    and emotions, 74
illness, 13, 54, 58
    and emotions, 54–5, 79
    as message, 111–12

S

sacrifice, 118–19
SAD (seasonal affective disorder), 25
sadness, 79, 80
schizophrenia, 25, 53
security, 2–3, 91–3, 99–100
self-discovery, 104–13, 121
self-doubt, and intuition, 43–6
self-expression, 110–11
    and logic, 62–3
self-worth, 116–17
sex, and instincts, 88
shadow, 77, 105, 109
shock, and emotions, 89
sleep disturbance, 80, 98
society
    and emotions, 78
    and fear, 31–2
solar plexus chakra, 82, 102–4 *and see* chakras
song/sing, 65, 98
Soul, 33–4, 95, 96 *and see* Higher Self
soul groups, 107–8
spiritual arrogance, 57, 116
spiritual path, 116
starvation, 107
stones (kidney and gall), 54
story, 76, 77
stress, 98–9
success, fear of, 110 *and see* fear
suffering, 60, 77–8
sun, 37, 58, 95
surrender, 93–4, 112, 123–4 *and see* letting go
survival, 87–100, 121, 124
    and fear, 92
    and illness, 96
    and instincts, 93–7
sweating, 54, 70, 88, 98
symbiotic relationships, 108–9 *and see* relationships

T

teachers, 8, 9, 32, 59–60
telepathy, 16

thalamus, 70
third eye, 38–9 *and under* chakras
thirst, 88
thoughts/thought forms, 15–19, 52, 71
throat chakra, 62, 103, 104 *and see* chakras
time, 117
tinnitus, 46
transformation, 58, 73, 85, 124
trauma, 89
trembling, 70, 98
trust, 32–3, 110
    and intuition, 32–3, 42–3
tumours, 54, 79

U
UFOs, 115
ulcers, stomach, 88
urge to pass urine, 54, 98

V
virtual reality, 102
visualisation, 41

W
wake-up call, 9
weeping, 98
whale, 24
wheezing, 98
wholeness, 4, 5, 37, 105
wisdom, exercises, 98–100
work, 7–8
worry, 54, 60, 61, 79, 84